SUNNY SIDE UP

Also by Susan Calman

*Cheer Up Love: adventures in depression
with the Crab of Hate*

SUNNY SIDE UP

a story of kindness and joy

SUSAN CALMAN

TWO
ROADS

First published in Great Britain in 2018 by Two Roads
An imprint of John Murray Press
An Hachette UK company

1

Copyright © Susan Calman 2018

The right of Susan Calman to be identified as the
Author of the Work has been asserted by her in accordance
with the Copyright, Designs and Patents Act 1988.

A CIP catalogue record for this title is available from the British Library

Hardback ISBN 9781473663862
eBook ISBN 9781473663893
Audio ISBN 9781473665712

Typeset in Sabon MT by Palimpsest Book Production Ltd, Falkirk, Stirlingshire

Printed and bound in Great Britain by Clays Ltd, Elcograf S.p.A.

Hodder & Stoughton policy is to use papers that are natural, renewable
and recyclable products and made from wood grown in sustainable forests.
The logging and manufacturing processes are expected to conform to the
environmental regulations of the country of origin.

Hodder & Stoughton Ltd
Carmelite House
50 Victoria Embankment
London EC4Y 0DZ

www.tworoadsbooks.com
www.hodder.co.uk

To everyone who's been Thelma to my Louise.
Thank you for driving over a few cliffs with me.
We always make it back safely.

CONTENTS

INTRODUCTION

OR HOW TO MANAGE EXPECTATIONS WITHOUT REALLY TRYING

THIS isn't an academic book and it certainly hasn't been heavily researched or funded. To be fair I did recently receive an honorary doctorate from Glasgow University, so technically I *am* a doctor. My sister, who spent five long years writing a PhD to get the same title, was delighted when I informed her of the honour being bestowed on me. On hearing the news, she shouted, 'I don't believe it,' and threw a mug across the room, which is surely the act of a happy sibling. I don't call myself 'Doctor Calman' in everyday life of course, because sadly it doesn't allow me to wander around a hospital trying to treat people. Heaven forbid someone should think I was a real medical professional instead of just a woman who has watched a lot of *Casualty*. I'd hate to find myself attempting to perform open-heart surgery using a grapefruit spoon.

What I'm trying to say is that before you read this book you should manage your expectations. My qualifications for spouting forth my views on the world are simply that I live here and I'm human. Just like you. Unless you happen to be a robot. If you are a sentient mechanical being can I say, on behalf of my fellow homo sapiens, thanks for reading this book instead of bringing about the end of the world like in the film *The Terminator*. Much appreciated. I don't fancy having to spend my Sunday battling cyborgs. Sunday is when I do the recycling.

You may be wondering what exactly you've got in your hands and I understand that. I've been wrestling with how to define this book myself, because I know at some point a journalist or interviewer will say, 'What's it all about, Susan?' and I like to be prepared for such scenarios. I always find that when I'm surprised by a question I panic and tend to shout out what I last had for dinner in an attempt to provide an answer. It may be an informative response but perhaps not the best tactic to increase sales. Imagine the scene. I'm on *Woman's Hour*, and Jenni Murray is staring me in the actual face, ready to interrogate me.

Jenni: So, can you describe to the listeners what the book is all about, Susan?

Me: [Stifled gurgle]

Jenni: Sorry, I didn't catch that.

Me: Macaroni cheese. With ready salted crisps on top. Never a slice of tomato, though. Tomato is wrong on macaroni cheese because it makes the crisps go soggy. A lot of people make macaroni cheese wrong . . .

Jenni: And that's all we have time for today; tomorrow we'll be talking about how to use cling film to increase confidence.

While that may well attract a lot of cheesy-pasta-loving readers, it wouldn't really reflect what you're about to read. Don't get me wrong – I do know some things about the content. For example, I absolutely know that this book won't solve all the problems of the world, so it's definitely not a panacea for the planet. Perhaps it's best described as a love letter to humanity. It's also in part a plea, a last-ditch attempt to persuade people to be better. You may be thinking, *How desperately arrogant, Susan; how dare you try and tell us what to do?* But I'm not ashamed to admit that I'm an optimist. It's hard work to continue to think happy thoughts but I truly believe that this planet and its inhabitants can still be amazing, can still be magnificent and can still be extraordinary.

I'd planned to write this book for some time but a series of convergent incidents persuaded me that I really had to. I'm a great believer in fate, due in part to my upbringing. My father's favourite expression is 'Whit's fur ye'll no' go by ye!' In very basic terms, that old Scots saying means 'What's meant to be will be.' I even have a mug that I drink my coffee out of in the morning with those very words emblazoned on it. Every time I don't get a job or I watch a television panel show that I've been rejected for I remember the saying and wait for the fates to decide my role in life. If it's right it'll happen. Hopefully.

Without getting all spiritual on you this early in the book, I truly believe that although we're all very much in control of our own destiny, that we can often make things happen through sheer determination, sometimes, for no discernible reason, we're given a nudge in the right direction. Whether it be dancing on the television as Wonder Woman or a chance encounter in a car park. Sometimes things simply must happen. And they often happen to me.

I was at the supermarket in Glasgow a year or so ago. My wife and I had finished our weekly shop, loaded the car up with cat food, beetroot and macaroni (we have a very interesting diet) and set off for home. As we turned the corner to exit the car park we saw an older woman (I won't use the term 'elderly' as that should only be used to describe trees, not people) who was resting against the boot of her car. She wasn't distressed or upset, she just looked tired. All *we* were about to do was go home and play *Assassin's Creed*, so we stopped the car to see how she was. Turned out she was fine but she was indeed tired, so we offered to do her shopping for her. After a lot of objections we did what any sensible person would do and bundled her into her car to wait for us. It probably looked slightly suspicious from afar but we were all having fun.

We bought her shopping, a bunch of flowers, wouldn't accept her money, made sure she was safely in her car and she drove off. A few weeks later my agent got an email from that lady's friend. She'd considered writing to the *Sunday Post* (a Scottish newspaper) to try to contact me, she said, but decided to try the Internet instead. The lady we'd helped was ninety-two and still going strong. She and her friends played bridge together every month and as I corresponded with her pal I learned a bit about their lives and their stories. I asked for their addresses and I started to send them postcards from my travels. As time progressed they would send me updates of how they thought I was doing on *Strictly* and I would give them some gossip from behind the scenes. Christmas greetings followed and in a spell of bad weather I contacted them to check they were OK and asked if they needed help with anything. In return I was told of family members' achievements and interesting books to read or music to listen to.

I tell you that story because it's so very simple. From that one act of kindness I have a group of friends who I would never have met in any other way. And that fills my heart with joy every day.

Over the past few years I've changed my life. I've gone from being miserable in the shadows to walking in the sunshine. I've most definitely turned my life Sunny Side Up.

So, if I'm asked to describe this book, I do know what to say. It's about two of the best things in the world: kindness and joy. And I, possibly the grumpiest woman in the world, am going to try and tell you why you need more of them in your life. Because I don't know about you, but I love a challenge.

DISCLAIMER

ONCE A LAWYER, ALWAYS A LAWYER

THIS book contains a lot of words and many of them come in the form of opinions. Those opinions are mine and mine alone and I often have little evidence for them apart from what's in my own head. In order to pre-empt some of the more obvious complaints I may receive, I'd like to make the following disclaimers to prevent angry social media interaction. I find that anticipation is often the best defence.

I make many sweeping generalisations in this book. I will happily tell you my thoughts on many subjects and offer little evidence to back them up. I offer no apology for such a gung-ho attitude; I just need you to know that's how I roll.

1. I never seek to deliberately offend anyone. So if at any point I use the wrong terminology or accidentally appear insensitive to any community I apologise in advance. If you think, *Was Susan being rude to me there?* I probably wasn't. If I want to offend you then you will definitely know about it.

2. Names, characters, businesses, places, events, locales and incidents are either the products of the author's imagination or used in a fictitious manner. Any resemblance to actual persons, living or dead, or actual events is purely coincidental. Unless they're clearly someone real. Then I am talking about them.

3. Don't get angry if you disagree with me. It's not worth it. It really isn't. If reading this book makes you apoplectic with rage and unable to function, then give it away. Don't stew over it. This day could be our last and there is little point in wasting it on me. Do something amazing, watch an old movie, have a laugh with friends. Use the book as a doorstop, or in the cat litter tray. I can't make you like me; I'm not a hormone.

4. I will contradict myself. Or I won't. See, I just did it there.

5. I will absolutely go off topic at times. Please remember this. If you're reading a chapter and suddenly think '*why is she talking about that?*' stay with me. I will always get back on track. I just really like getting to my destination via the scenic route.

Please address all complaints to me on social media using the hashtag #SusanRocksMyWorld. I don't often look at my mentions but if you use that I'll definitely see your comments.

Nothing like starting a book on kindness and joy with a legal disclaimer, is there? You know what they say: once a lawyer, always a boring, risk-averse idiot. Enjoy.

CHAPTER 1
THE BEGINNING:

I GUESS YOU'RE WONDERING WHY
I CALLED YOU ALL HERE?

YOU may have been given this book as a present. Or you may have liked the cover. Or you may have recognised my face from the television. Perhaps it was a charity shop impulse buy, or more likely it's the year 2057 and you've found this in the barren wasteland that used to be planet earth. Only copies of my book, cockroaches and Boots Advantage Cards survived the rise of the machines (*The Terminator* will happen) but however you've found it, I hope you enjoy what you're about to read.

Being honest with you, I always like the start of a book. Some writers are frightened of a blank page but I find it fascinating. To be fair, this book is non-fiction so it's not as difficult to kick off as one set in the realms of fantasy. Fiction is trickier. I've always wondered how I'd start my made-up magnum opus, which is incidentally a detective novel set in Glasgow starring a woman who has a lot of cats (look, it's non-fiction, OK!). I have dabbled with the first few chapters, but I always struggle to find that intriguing first sentence which will hook the reader in. The best I've come up with so far is . . .

It was a normal Monday morning and Greta Foolsam slurped her seventh coffee of the day, lit her pipe and looked out of the window to the busy street below. 'Damn!' she exclaimed. Because there he was. Staring at her from outside the pound shop. The pound shop that used to be a Woolworths. God, she missed the pick 'n' mix. The taste of the foam bananas against her tongue of a morning. But there he was. Then he wasn't. There was a knock at the door. Greta put her sensible brogues back on, adjusted her beret and strode like a young Katharine Hepburn to the front door. Through the glass she could see an outline. She squinted against the sun, but there it was. A penguin. A giant penguin.

I know – it's amazing. This book you're reading now, though, isn't set in the gritty world of pound shops; this book is all real. Well, as real as any memoir can be; it's certainly written from my perspective, so it's tainted I suppose, but the veracity of my recollections would almost certainly stand up in court. The victors write history and books are written by strange, solitary individuals who want to narrate books about giant penguins. I like to think that my books reflect who I am: contradictory, written in the moment and almost certainly annoying to some people.

By way of introduction, let me explain a few things. This book here is my second book; *Cheer Up Love* was my first foray into the writing world and was principally about the fact that I have depression. It was an honest, sometimes funny, but rather raw retelling of how I deal with my own head. It was my way of trying to explain to the world how it feels when the darkness descends, and everything seems to be downright awful. If you haven't read the book, please don't worry. It's not prescribed reading, and anything you need to know will be included in this book. If you watch *Die Hard 2: Die Harder*, it's a fair bet that you'll be able to understand what's happening without too much bother. But for any of you who are feeling nervous about jumping in at stage two of the Calman revolution, let me summarise what you need to know – like an American drama series where they remind you of relevant plot points at the start of every episode.

In broad terms:

I have depression and have had it for almost as long as I can remember. *Cheer Up Love* was about that. It's a cheerful book about depression. Honestly.

1. I have desperately low self-confidence.

2. I dislike the way that I look.

3. I like lists.

4. I love cats.

5. I'm constantly evaluating the human condition.

6. I wish I was a little bit taller.

7. I'm oddly optimistic despite thinking that the world is awful.

8. I'm aware that sometimes I get carried away with things and my thought process can be rather confusing.

9. I like to make absolute statements without much proof or research.

10. I used to be a lawyer but gave it all up to become a comedian. I know. There's nothing you can say that my mum hasn't already.

11. Almost all of my references relate to television from the 1980s. If you don't understand what I'm referring to in some of the chapters please feel free to use the Internet to catch up.

Oh, and I'm gay. Hence the occasional references to my wife. I'm fine with it and hopefully you are too. It's just the way it is. If you have a problem with that fact, then please feel free to exchange this book for something you find more suitable. I don't mind. I'd rather you were happy.

Since I wrote *Cheer Up Love* lots of things have changed. For a start I've aged. That's not surprising I suppose, it's just what happens. What is slightly more surprising is that it's not just my face or my rapidly greying hair that's altered; *I've* changed as a person. Genuinely changed. I've embraced my mental upgrade, and the very act of writing my first book was partly what inspired me to try new things and push myself outside my comfort zone. If you've read *Cheer Up Love* you'll know that I enjoy everything being exactly the same all the time. But that's a highly annoying character trait, and not just for me. My loved ones often tire of my foibles. I'd be happy to eat the same meal every day, wear the same clothes and go to the same pub. But that requirement for familiarity comes from a fear, a paralysing terror of anything different. It turns out that living that way is quite dull, and the stomach-churning feeling of jumping outside a comfort zone can be quite exhilarating. I was doing OK, I was managing – coping well, even – but I was missing something vitally important from my life. Joy. I was cruising along but I wasn't truly happy because it was safer in many ways not to be.

But then in 2017 I did something quite peculiar, which changed my life, probably forever. And it was something that made me rather evangelical about having fun, lightening up and feeling the absolute rush of excitement that can come from true happiness.

In my first book I talked about suggestions people had made to help me with my depression, one of which was to dance. I said this:

'I can't dance, so all I really expressed was the fact that I hated the fact I couldn't dance. Also, I don't know if you've ever tried to throw the shape of the emotion caused by someone writing something offensive about the way you look on an Internet forum, but it's not easy.'

This particular paragraph has been quoted back at me often on social media in recent months and so I'll be honest: I am quite happy to retract that statement in full because recent events have empirically proven it wrong. Because I managed to dance for ten weeks in the BBC show *Strictly Come Dancing*, which, if you're one of my international readers, is the equivalent of *Dancing with the Stars*. I cha-cha'd and quickstepped my heart out and lasted far longer than I think anyone would have thought possible. Most importantly, by the time I left the show I was a very different person to the one who'd started it.

But this book isn't all about *Strictly* because I'd started writing this book long before I entered the be-glittered world of dance. For the past couple of years I've felt an irresistible urge to do something very simple. I want to change the world. *Strictly* was a happy accident that added to my mission, but I've inhabited this planet for forty-three years (at the time of writing) and I've become increasingly upset at the way things are going – like a BBC drama that's brilliant to start with, but by episode three you're throwing things at the television in frustration. Fear, anger, rude behaviour, intolerance, spite and bullying are all in evidence every single day of the week. But I believe that if we were all a little bit kinder, a little bit more full of joy, things would be better.

Sometimes things come together wonderfully, like Cagney and Lacey or baked potatoes and butter. And so *Strictly Come Dancing* melted beautifully into my theories of how to make the world a better place. It was as if I was living through an experiment full of glitter and sequins.

As I danced, kindness and joy shone through from the people I met, the people who watched the show and strangers who became friends.

So, this is my *Calmanifesto of Happiness*. I hope you enjoy it. And I really hope it makes you feel better.

CHAPTER 2
KINDNESS:
WHAT IS IT?
AND WHY DO WE NEED IT?

I'M a very old-fashioned gal. I state that because sometimes people think I'm far more 'alternative' than I actually am. Yes, I gave up a highly paid job as a corporate lawyer to become a stand-up comedian. Yes, I'm married to a woman. And yes, I do think that packet white sauce is superior to a homemade roux, but apart from these obvious eccentricities I'm actually very traditional.

I was brought up to have manners, to respect my elders, to say please and thank you. If my family had a mantra it would be 'Make sure you don't bother anyone.' While I'm quite happy that some of the more repressive aspects of Victorian Britain are now obsolete (for a start I'm allowed to get married now), and I don't sit in my leather wingback chair of an evening shouting about how things were much better back in the day, I have become quite uneasy about the way society is moving.

I yearn for the time when you could leave your door open and kids could play in the street. I want to hold on to that idealistic view of life and yes, maybe it didn't exist everywhere in the country, but hey. Don't stop a girl from dreaming. In many ways the past few years have felt like the start of a horror movie. That slow but discernible feeling one gets when watching a cheap slasher flick on the television. Things are about to go horribly wrong, but no one seems to notice. Why did they go into the basement? Why did they swim in the sea at three in the morning in the nude? Why did they wander into an empty house in Texas that had chainsaw marks on the door?

The thing that I value in life more than anything else is kindness. A kind person is the most attractive person in the world. I fell in love with my wife the moment I saw her because she seemed to have the kindest face I'd ever seen. And I was right. She is kind. Sometimes overly so: she's the type of person who will take a photograph for someone and end up inviting them to Christmas dinner. In many ways my kindness comes from her. You may not believe this (and many don't) but I'm an extremely shy person, I really am. People are often confused when they meet me in real life and are confronted by a shuffling woman who doesn't seem to resemble the confident, flirtatious person they've just seen on stage. So, when audience members would come up to me after a show or stop me in a shop and try to speak to me I would simply walk away rather than have to chat to them. My wife, the personification of kindness, took me aside one day and, in the incredibly sensitive way that she has, told me that I was being an arse. She reminded me that my awkwardness with social encounters was irrelevant compared to the feelings of the people who'd come up to speak to me.

She asked me a simple question: 'How would you feel if someone you really admired was rude to you, irrespective of the reasons why?' And she was right. Because I had once dared to make a similar approach, in the dim and distant past.

Many years ago, when I'd just started out in comedy, I went to an awards ceremony. It was a very relaxed affair: a few drinks in a bar, some perspex trophies and lots of comics of varying ability and fame all milling about together. I was standing at the bar minding my own business when I saw my comedy idol. Victoria Wood. It's difficult for me to put into words what she meant to me; for years she was everything I wanted to be. And she still is.

I first saw her on *An Audience with Victoria Wood*, a TV special that was made in 1988. I'm sure it was on in the background while the fourteen-year-old me grumped around the house, but for some reason someone in my family recorded it on a VHS tape. I watched it again, and again, and again, and again until I was word perfect. I knew every movement, the cadence, the laughter breaks and the expressions. I can truthfully say that nothing has made me laugh as much since. I properly laughed at her routines and songs, bent over and crying in pain because I just couldn't stop. I even loved the bits I didn't quite understand. For example, I had no idea why the notion of escaping from a room by knotting together sheets to make a moped was funny. But it was. I saw her at the Royal Albert Hall when she performed for fifteen nights and, for me, it was as exciting as seeing Elvis or Madonna. And as I grew up watching her it was clear that it wasn't just comedy that she excelled at. *Pat and Margaret* was one of the most touching pieces of television I've seen, and with her companion Julie Walters she proved that she was a creative genius across so many genres.

She was my funny friend at a time when I needed one. I was lonely as a teenager, with few mates, but I didn't need them when I had Victoria on my side. More than that: when I saw her perform I knew, as that lonely fourteen-year-old, what it was that I wanted to do with my life. I wanted to stand in front of a microphone and make people laugh. Just like her.

For most of the intervening thirty years since I saw that first TV show, any close relationship I've made is based on the answer to one simple question: 'Do you know "The Ballad of Barry and Freda"?' If the person answers in the negative, then that tends to be the end of our dealings. In my opinion, if you can't shout 'Beat me on the bottom with a *Woman's Weekly*!' at the top of your voice then you haven't lived. It wasn't just me that she touched though; Victoria's writing became part of the public's consciousness in a wonderful, understated way. I was in a tearoom on a small Scottish island not that long ago and the service was slow to say the least. One by one the courses were brought to us by a shuffling waitress and tipped slowly onto the table. The only customers were myself and my wife and one other table of hungry patrons. As my order was placed in front of me after some considerable time, I heard the woman at the other table very quietly say, 'And another soup.' We silently high fived each other, then turned back to our respective companions.

It was only when I became a stand-up myself that I truly appreciated how good she was. Her writing is so specific and detailed that every word counts. She wouldn't go on stage and wing it; she knew exactly what she wanted to say and how she wanted to say it. And watching her taught me a valuable lesson: that things could be funnier if you changed a word, or a descriptive term.

But there she was. A few feet away from me. And I froze. I stood shaking in my shoes, afraid to approach her. Not because she was being stand-offish – far from it. She was standing in the middle of the room quite happily chatting away. Eventually one of my friends became annoyed at my lack of action, went over to her and told her I was a big fan. I walked over, squeaked something about loving her and someone took a picture of us. She was delightful, given that there was a tiny sweating woman beside her. Sadly, I can't find that picture now. It was in the days before iClouds and back-ups. I suppose I thought I had time to meet her again. It sometimes makes me quite weepy when I realise I never will.

My wife was right (as she almost unfailingly is), so I always remember Victoria Wood's kindness whenever someone approaches me and tells me that they like what I do. I now stand up straight and smile, even if in the depths of my soul I want to run away. It's trite to say so but kindness costs nothing (unless you're buying someone a car or something) and it can affect people in a way that you can never imagine. That one meeting was one of the most special moments of my life and I'll treasure it forever.

I really started to think about kindness after writing *Cheer Up Love*. Examining what I'd written after a hiatus gave me one startling insight: I was angry a lot of the time. And much of this anger was directed at the world; I felt increasingly and unsustainably full of rage about what was happening around me. I found myself seething in the morning after being awake for mere minutes after a brief glimpse at social media or listening to morning radio shows. A bleak cloud above me dimming any sunshine in my life. In my typically analytical fashion I sat down to try and work out what it was that had changed, why I found myself so at odds with the world in which I was living. And there was one thing that stood out for me like a giant penguin. A devaluation of kindness.

It's probably useful, at this point, to clarify what I mean by this. If there's one lesson I've learned in life it's that words can mean very different things to different people.

Fundamentally, kindness is the quality of being friendly and generous. Considerate even. But in many ways that's an oversimplified definition of something that's tremendously complicated. Kindness can be spontaneous or planned. Kindness can be cruel, and sometimes intentionally so. There is undoubtedly a school of thought that believes it's better to be brutally honest to people because it's much worse to lie to them. I've never thought anything that upsets others is particularly kind. I've always believed that a kind gesture should have a positive impact of some sort. Of course, there's always a point where someone should be put out of their misery. I said to my wife the other day that I was going to give up my job to become a professional darts player. In a very kind way she told me to shut up.

Thus I hesitate to provide you with an absolute definition of what kindness is. Absolute definitions are part of the problem these days. You're gay or straight, black or white, anti- or pro-Brexit, left- or right-wing. The shades of what make us interesting disappear as the tribal nature of society emerges. But in order to make this book work, I suppose I have to set out what I think kindness and joy are.

For me the essence of kindness is where it stems from; what the intention behind the kind act is. One of the unfortunate remnants of my legal training is that I'm always looking to define something in ways that would apply in court, but this can be a useful process. Think of kindness as a 'good crime', if you will. Apart from some strict liability offences, in order to be convicted of a crime you have to have both the *mens rea* and the *actus reus*. The *actus reus* is the actual doing of something – for example in a kind act, it would be the giving of a present or picking up a wallet that you've found in the street. The *mens rea* is the mental element of a crime: the direct intention of doing something. Kindness is, in some ways, simply the reverse of a criminal act. Have you done something that's had a positive impact on someone, and did you mean to do it? Then you've done something kind.

That's not to say that kindness can't be unintentional but this book's agenda is to persuade people to be intentionally kind. To mean it. So while, for example, me not entering *Britain's Got Talent* with my cat/human circus group called 'Calman and the Catrobats' is a kindness to the other competitors, it isn't a deliberate act of kindness. I just don't have the time to make leotards for the cats.

So, the first element of being kind is the intention of making something better for someone. The second part is the proviso that you don't *need* to do it: nothing legally or contractually compels you to act in a certain way, but you feel you should. This is, obviously, subjective to some extent. I'm aware that people have different views on what's expected of them. I've lost count of the number of times I've heard men say that they're 'babysitting' their own children. As if being at home and looking after their descendants is some great kindness to their wives, as opposed to what they should be doing anyway.

Kindness isn't something you're obliged to do because of an employment contract or a law. At best it's the gut instinct inside all of us that tells us what we should do. The empathy part of us that spots someone in need and resolves to do something about it.

And that, to me, is the essence of why kindness is so important in the world right now: empathy. Harper Lee in *To Kill a Mockingbird* wrote, 'You never really understand a person until you consider things from his point of view . . . Until you climb inside of his skin and walk around in it.'

While I'm not in any way advocating that you kidnap and skin a stranger, the experience of understanding another person's condition from their perspective is crucial. Placing yourself in their shoes and feeling what they are feeling. In that way you can feel pain and hope and joy.

In some ways it's about being a mind reader, which is actually easier than you might think.

I've been fascinated by mind readers and spiritualists for years, ever since I learned of the Fox sisters, a group of women who were instrumental in the birth of spiritualism. They used a series of noises to indicate that they were communicating with spirits and were much feted in society as the real deal. It turned out that they weren't communicating with the dead; rather, they were contorting and cracking their joints to create an unearthly sound that fooled many of those who went to their séances.

Oddly enough, in a way this interest in spiritualism led to my career in comedy. While I appreciate that plenty of people believe in life after death and communication from beyond the grave, many of those who've claimed to be mediums are, actually, just incredible empaths. They can look at someone and, from the changes in expression and their body language, make educated guesses about whether they're on the right or wrong track; they can tell if they've hit a nerve or if they're way off target. The best comedians are empaths. They know if a joke is hitting the mark and not just by the laughter, but by the way the laughter sounds, the looks on people's faces and the way the room moves as one.

The key to empathy is to look at someone. To *really* look at them. Not a cursory glance, and not a strange penetrating gaze either. There's a middle ground where you can properly see someone. Communicate with them. Read their minds, so to speak. That's often why an unexpected kind gesture really hits home. *How did they know?*

I didn't say that I needed help. I didn't ask for this. It's because someone has paid attention, has noticed and has listened.

It's quite astonishing how much effort it takes to pay attention to someone for a prolonged period of time though. My brain is now so trained to think of several things at the one time that slowing it down can feel painful. I'm as guilty as the next person of having a conversation with a friend, looking in their eyes as they tell me a story from their life while in my head all I'm thinking is *'I wonder how you make mackerel pate, I must look that up in a minute, but then I'd have to buy mackerel and maybe an avocado, and I had an avocado but it went off, like those raspberries I bought, why don't I eat fruit? I should go to the gym, last time I went to the gym someone scraped my car, I should get a new car, maybe a van like in the A-Team, I wonder if they still show the A-Team anywhere? Is there a market for Soldiers of Fortune these days?'*. I'm a brilliant friend.

In my mind the advent of recent technology has made this brain hopping more prevalent. I'm happy to admit that I'm as much of a tech fiend as the next middle-aged lesbian, but I know what it's doing to us. Mobile phones packed with apps, I need to tweet what I'm doing, I should be Instagramming this coffee . . . Even when we're talking we're thinking about the next thing, the next text and the next post.

The older I get the more I hate mobile phones and what they've done to us. I went to Florence with my wife and, as you do, looked up the must-see locations in the city.

One of them was the Uffizi Gallery, filled to the brim with art and sculpture and history. We dutifully filed into the museum ready to be overwhelmed by what we saw. As we wandered the corridors past the da Vincis and the Caravaggios there was one common theme: very few people were actually looking at the pictures. They were taking pictures of the pictures. As I stood in front of Botticelli's *The Birth of Venus* I stood watching the crowd, who in turn stood, phones out, not even looking at what they were taking a photo of.

I'm sure that some of those people will go home and pore over every detail of the paintings, looking at the composition and the brush strokes and marvelling at the imagery and subtle hidden meanings. Just as many will probably stick the pic on their Facebook page with the same amount of care as the picture of the spaghetti that they had for lunch. They don't see anything. They don't look at anything. Everything is second-hand, even opinions. I had a conversation with a mate at the end of last year about the new *Star Wars* film. When I asked my friend whether she liked it, she replied that the *Guardian* had given it a fair review. 'But did YOU like it?' I asked again. What followed was a number of different reviews and opinions from various Internet message boards and websites that formed an opinion about the movie. She couldn't actually tell me if she liked it. It was as though she was afraid to have an opinion in case it was 'wrong'. I told her exactly what I thought. That I mostly enjoyed it but I was slightly disappointed with some aspects. The silence that followed was deafening. No, I hadn't read the

Telegraph, or looked on Rotten Tomatoes. I'd watched the film. And it was OK.

You might not have given it much thought before, but I suspect you have your own definition of what kindness is. It might be different to mine, but that's OK. For the purposes of this book, kindness is a deliberate act, which involves other people (that you may or may not know personally), and some form of action or thought bringing about a positive result.

It's a bit of a ramshackle definition but it works. Goodness me, I do love putting together a ramshackle theory. You can see now why the kindest thing I ever did for my clients was to stop being a lawyer.

CHAPTER 3

JOY: HAPPINESS BY ANY OTHER NAME WOULD SMELL AS SWEET

THIS book is about two discernible things, kindness and joy. Kindness is in many ways the easier topic to write about because, as a concept, it's easier to understand. It's something one can create with a positive action, whereas joy is a very personal thing, a feeling that can be generated by others or created internally. Joy also changes with age. What makes one scream with delight at the age of eight seems meaningless through the passage of time, and so to isolate and define it is tough. That's what makes it so delightful, though, because joy can surprise me in ways that I still find rather magical. And in the same way, witnessing the joy of others can be truly magnificent.

To me joy is more than happiness; it's a sudden rush of excitement and pride and emotion that can last a millisecond or an hour. An unexplainable part of the human mind that obliterates the bad and only accepts the good. Like when the *Millennium Falcon* jumps into hyperspace in *Star Wars*, the mind shoots forward joy and transports us to a primal place where nothing but wonder exists.

One of the reasons I love joy is that the thing that gives you that feeling is different for everyone. When I was much younger I got the most amazing Christmas present ever. I'm going to say I was ten – mainly because I can't remember how old I was, but ten seems appropriate. In almost all of my childhood stories I'm ten; it makes things easier. So, when I was ten I got an unexpected gift. Every year we got to browse the Argos catalogue and choose a present. Santa would then know what we'd chosen (because we would send him a letter) and if we weren't total idiots for the rest of the year, on Christmas morning those presents would be waiting for us in the living room.

This particular year I got a portable record player. It played 45s, 33s and 78s. The sound quality was terrible, the records jumped if someone shut their car door at the end of the street but oh my gosh, the feeling when I opened that present. I hadn't asked for it, you see. It was an extra, a surprise and I felt like the coolest girl in school. You could pick it up and walk around with it! And that's what I did. I used to pack that record player up and walk around the house with it for no reason other than that I could. It was one of the first times in my life that I can remember feeling joy as opposed to contentment or happiness. I'm sure I had moments of excitement before, but this was different. This one connected everything into one ball of happiness. And even the memory of that player, of sitting on my bedroom floor' playing the 7-inch single of Madonna's 'Into the Groove, makes me smile. Residual joy may be less potent but it's no less fun.

People talk of feeling joy when their child is born or

when they get married but even a simple rush of happiness in smaller doses is incredible. The most mundane event can fill your mind with positivity. And often, as you get older, it's the practical that brings the most joy. Finding that the milk in the fridge is still in date when you thought it might not be. Making the earlier train home. A cat falling asleep on you and snoring for hours.

I remember the first time I felt proper adult joy – and I don't mean anything saucy by that, I mean the first time I experienced happiness because of something responsible and grown-up. I'm slightly ashamed to say that I put off being a responsible citizen for some time. Even after I left my student digs and bought my first flat I didn't wholly buy into being a grown-up. I don't know if it scared me a little bit or if I just couldn't be bothered, but shopping was done in a haphazard fashion. I ran out of cleaning products regularly, and more often than I care to remember I'd be running to the supermarket on a Monday morning for the most basic of supplies. I am strangely contradictory in that I'm desperately organised (some would say a control freak) when it comes to some parts of my life, but in others I'm like a five-year-old child left alone to plan a household. That all changed when I met my wife. She's organised in the aspects of life that I don't care about. In fact when I first met her she rather terrified me. The shirts in her wardrobe were ordered first by use (work/smart casuals/casual/fancy), then by colour (black to white with gradients in between). I notoriously used the floor to store my clothes and while at first I detested the new regime, I learned to appreciate it – and more than that, enjoy it.

This may sound stupid, but we have toilet rolls now. Lots of them. In a large toilet-roll box that is in an airing cupboard. I have never once run out of toilet rolls, and that makes me so happy. I have not one but two medicine cabinets that my wife has arranged (surprise!) from top left (head pills) to bottom right (blister plasters). I can find anything I want in seconds. She does a regular shop at the chemist so we don't run out and the cabinets are full to the brim with potions and ointments. Bite cream – yes, burn dressings – of course, vitamins that have never been opened – absolutely. Opening the cabinets makes me smile every time, because I'm a grown-up who can locate ear-wax-softening oil at a moment's notice (top shelf, just beside the painkillers). It brings me joy, and while it may be silly to some, to me it's a sign of stability, and even of love. That someone cares for me so much that they spend time arranging a cabinet – two cabinets! – full of things to make me feel better.

That's the bottom line, you see: joy is an acutely personal emotion and can be set off by anything. For example, smells can trigger joy. It's trite to say it, I know, but the aroma of fresh coffee wafting through the house makes me so happy. My cats' paws can smell like digestive biscuits and I could sniff them all day long. Of course, senses can also trigger negative feelings, especially those related to matters of the heart. Love is a strange thing; it's a state of mind that can be distressing and hopeful in the same millisecond and I've never known anything else in my life that brings such great joy and then such utter disappointment. Apart from *Miss Congeniality* (brilliant) and *Miss*

Congeniality 2: Armed and Fabulous (awful). Scientists may say that love is simply a matter of biology or chemistry or some such stuff, but science can't explain why love lingers in our memories far longer than it should.

I was on the train the other day and suddenly felt completely and utterly sick. The effect was so immediate that I genuinely thought I would vomit on myself. Oddly, the cause of my nausea wasn't the smell of the toilet; it was the overpowering scent of Dewberry that was clinging for dear life to a fellow passenger. To be fair to the Body Shop it's not that I have a particular gripe against the fragrance; what makes me hate it is the fact that it brings back memories of my first ever love. OK, 'love' may be stretching it slightly; it was more of a teenage infatuation. And if I'm very honest it was less infatuation and more gratitude. You see, the woman who drenched herself in Dewberry was the woman with whom I shared my first proper kiss. What I remember most of all about her isn't the kiss itself – I suspect the event was rather rushed and probably more awkward than enjoyable. No, my abiding memory is that she had everything Dewberry: hand cream, foot cream, shower gel. You could almost see the scent wafting around her like the old Bisto advert.

And that's what made me feel sick when I caught a whiff of it in the train, because the overwhelming emotion when I think of that time is humiliation. She dumped me shortly after the kiss even though, in truth, there was no real relationship to be dumped from. But it hurt like hell at the time and even now, over twenty years later, the smell of Dewberry makes me feel like a complete loser.

For similar reasons, I refuse to allow incense into my house, because even the most cursory sniff of the stuff reminds me of the first woman I slept with. She was, I suppose, my first love in the truest sense – although once again gratitude was certainly part of the reason I fell for her. She loved incense; I suspect she would have filled an inhaler with incense if she could have. And then, in a pattern that was to continue for several years, she also dumped me, this time in true lesbian-drama circumstances. Less than twenty-four hours after we'd first fooled around, an event that I was still delirious with joy about, she called me and asked if she'd left her girlfriend's gloves at my house. Which led me to ask the awkward question, 'But I thought I was your girlfriend?' I learned a valuable lesson that day – don't get naked without asking a few questions of the person you're getting naked with. So this is why I hate incense: because it reminds me of trying to rip a payphone off the wall of a student flat in 1993 while shouting, 'She can shove her fucking gloves up her fucking arse.'

Oddly enough, however, even though the smell of the Dewberry triggered such a negative reaction, in a small way it also made me feel joyous. Because that first kiss, that first love is part of what makes me who I am now. The building blocks to the Calman who can now look back at some of the worst times with a shrug.

We all have things that we know, or think, will bring us joy and that is brilliant. Actually, I'm so enthused by the concept of joy that I'm going to put a health warning on this next part of the chapter because it might make people feel sick. And believe me, the fact that I'm scribbling this saccharine nonsense is as much of a surprise to me as it is to anyone else. I'm the grumpy woman who stands at her window shouting at people who make too much noise in the street. I'm the one who gets annoyed at people who skip the queue or who don't understand the etiquette of remaining completely silent in a lift. But maybe that makes me exactly the kind of person to truly understand the nature of joy and how wonderful it is. Because for so very long I've been avoiding it I've chased it out of my life so I could carry on being a depressed, miserable woman who sneers at happiness. My turnaround is nothing less than a *"Road to Damascus"* moment. I imagine it's like finding God later in life, a realisation that everything you knew before has completely changed.

So why is it important to feel joy? The answer is simple: because it's amazing. Like a Disney cartoon brimming with unicorns dancing and rainbow houses and rabbits wearing trousers. It's as essential to life as breathing, or eating, and without it life would be almost unbearable. Joy is a necessary point of respite from the almost never-ending parade of depressing events that seems to fill newspapers and general conversation. It's the moment when the colour kicks in after the sepia-toned misery at the beginning of *The Wizard of Oz*, the forgotten ten-pound note in a winter coat. Often sudden, often unexpected and always incredible.

It's important that we still feel joy, and perpetuate it, because without it the world would be a terrible place.

But the greatest thing about joy is that while the pleasure

may initially be felt by just one person, it's also infectious, like a happiness-transmitted disease (HTD). When you see someone enthralled by a moment of joy, it spreads like wildfire, unexpectedly lifting the mood further than you could imagine. The most common word that was used about my time on *Strictly* was 'joyous' and I received hundreds of emails and letters from viewers who said that watching my happiness made them happy. To see someone having such a wonderful time meant that for a short while *they* felt that positivity and rush of endorphins. And that feeling wasn't make-believe for me; I can only remember a few other moments in my life where I've been happier than I was dancing with Kevin Clifton on a Saturday night. The week that we quickstepped to 'Bring Me Sunshine' was almost too much for my mind to cope with. Not only was that song the first dance at my wedding but it is also, in my view, the happiest song in the world. The lyrics are everything. Sadly, for copyright reasons, I can't reproduce them in this book but if you have a moment to think of them please do. Close your eyes and hum the tune, go on. I dare you not to smile while you're doing it.

Immediately after we finished performing the quickstep live on Saturday night, as I stood with a top hat in my hand and a smile as wide as the River Clyde on my face, I realised that for years I hadn't been allowing my brain to feel that feeling; my self-esteem was so low that to be truly happy was inconceivable. But when I let that joy in, it was the best and most utterly glorious thing I've done.

My wife said something the other day that has stayed

with me. She said that the thing she missed most about *Strictly* was 'Saturday Susan'. I must have looked puzzled, so she explained. For years she's known me as a rather depressed (but still lovely) woman who more often than not would see the worst-case scenario in all situations. I've even made up a whole theory about it – Calman's Law. This is a new sociological term that I've coined myself. In essence it is 'The worst thing that could possibly happen, no matter how unlikely, will happen to Susan Calman.'

I have a sixth sense for things. You know at the start of an episode of *Casualty* you have a sense of unease because you're certain that the man on the tractor will get horrifically injured? Not by falling into the tractor – that's too obvious. No, at some point he will go the shops or something, trip over a poodle and fall head first into a paper-shredder.

That's how I used to feel all the time. But when I was dancing, my wife saw someone else. Someone who was happy. Someone who was full of joy. And it made *her* happy. It had given her an HTD. And she told me bluntly that she wants Saturday Susan every day of the week. And so, while I'm writing this book as an appeal to you, dear readers, to find more joy in your life, please know that I'm trying to do the same. Because when you open up to joy, it really does bring sunshine. And not just to you.

CHAPTER 4
THE STATE OF THE NATION

WHY WE NEED KINDNESS

DO you know what I think the country needs? A state of
the nation address. But not one given by the Prime Minister,
the Leader of the Opposition or indeed any politician or
person in a position of power. Because let's face it, we
sort of know what they're going to say, don't we? Yes,
things are tough, yes things might get worse but if we all
muck in everything will be fine. Everyone should stop
being critical and get on board with [insert name of party
in power here] and their plans to make things better. And
besides, it's not their fault it's all gone wrong – we should
blame the last government/Europe/immigrants/potatoes.
Perhaps it's the inevitability of their response that makes
me less keen to listen to people in power. The 'stiff upper
lip', the 'Let's all just get on with things and stop moaning'
attitude that stifles discourse.

I'm so used to platitudes that when I hear a politician
tell me what the world is like, I have a tendency to switch
off. Long speeches at party conferences sound like the
teacher in Charlie Brown telling a story: 'Wah wah wah'

ad infinitum. I think I also have a slight suspicion that those in power don't really know what's actually happening, or that they choose to ignore it. Because if you don't know that something exists, then it's not real, is it? I know that's a huge, sweeping generalisation and that there are many elected members of Parliament and devolved Houses who do care and who do pay attention, but there are definitely some who appear to pay as much attention to reality as a unicorn in the Emerald City. I most certainly understand the popularly held view that those involved in politics have stopped caring, perhaps because the problems we have are so entrenched, but also because it sometimes feels that politicians are hoping the problems will go away if they ignore them for long enough.

But that doesn't work, and ignoring something can just make it worse. I should know. I've been ignored on countless occasions and that just makes me more determined to be heard. In fact, nothing makes me angrier than someone dismissing my opinions out of hand. Social media means that we have more outlets to express our concerns and vent our frustration, but without any possibility of effecting real change, it can feel as useful as standing at a bus stop at midnight screaming into the night.

It may seem childish to suggest that something as simple as more kindness and joy might save the world – I get that. I don't expect for a second that politicians just being nicer to each other and to us will suddenly make the world a better place. But we can change things. I can change and I can try and persuade others to do the same. The point of difficulty, as with almost everything, is that in order to make a difference we have to *want* to do so. I wanted to give up smoking for years but still wanted to smoke. In very simple terms it didn't matter how many times I muttered about my desire to be free from my addiction; until I actually did something about it, I carried on smoking. We can all talk an extremely good game, but to actually play takes a lot more energy.

I often think of my kindness and joy Calmanifesto in the middle of the night when struck by insomnia. I frequently can't sleep and find myself awake at 3 a.m. scheming and planning the future of the world. Or I end up down a YouTube rabbit hole of conspiracy theories about JFK, or the Moon Landings or even the Loch Ness Monster, which terrify and fascinate me in equal measure. Not being able to sleep is a curious thing: when the body is so tired that one moment it's impossible to keep your eyes open, and the next moment you feel like you couldn't be more awake. The early hours are the times that I often find myself most able to think, looking out into the pitch dark, trying not to make any noise so as not to wake the family. As a result, some of my ideas are fairly impossible; often stupid but always well-intentioned. And to a sleep-deprived Calman they sound brilliant.

At 3 a.m. the simple act of listening to the public seems like a particularly good idea. I mean *really* listening to them, not taking a series of tweets as evidence because let's face it, despite what many would like us to think, the majority of the population are neither on Twitter nor do they care about it. It's easy to believe that the whole world is stuck to a computer screen all day scanning Twitter for the latest scandal or political fight, but they aren't. They really aren't. About 65 million people live in the UK and, according to research, approximately 17.1 million of those are on Twitter in 2018. Many more people use Facebook, but statistics don't take note of the amount these social media accounts are used, or indeed of multiple accounts. Suffice to say that an opinion expressed on social media is no substitute for actually allowing someone to talk for an extended period of time.

So it's possibly an unworkable suggestion, but part of me believes that instead of listening to politicians and PR people all the time, someone unexpected should be allowed to say what they think of the world we live in. Every month someone new should be chosen at random to stand up, give us their state of the nation address and provide some suggestions as to what they think would make things better. A teacher from Wolverhampton, a doctor from Aberdeen or a pensioner from Derby. Everyone has a different view on how the world is right now; some are content, many more are probably not. But let's hear them. Properly hear them.

Naturally, there might be some who violently rail against the left or the right, who have nothing more than anger to report, but just as many may have sensible ideas and solutions to present. If nothing else, it would let people feel heard. The impotence of silence can be the most frustrating feeling of all. And perhaps it would help us feel kinder towards our fellow citizens if we listened to their voices and heard about their lives.

You may be reading this thinking, *What a useless idea, Susan – imagine giving over valuable time to people who I don't care about*, and if you are then I can understand your cynicism. I used to voraciously devour the news – every paper, every broadcast and every documentary and radio show going. Now I don't. In the morning I get up, make a pot of coffee and listen to podcasts about films or comedy or Agatha Christie – anything other than what's actually happening in the world. Sadly I can't completely avoid it – I'm on social media a lot and I hear conversations in the pub and on trains – but there's one constant in all of it: people are pissed off. Disgruntled. Annoyed. Not all the time – we've not reached the level of disgust that means people have taken to the streets, or lost a sense of who we are – but it's there, an undercurrent of unease, and it's getting stronger.

Political discourse, which has always been packed with dispute and aggression, has, now more than at any other time that I can remember, become distressing. You see, kindness isn't just about doing someone's shopping or paying them a compliment; it's about a holistic approach to humanity. It's about an attempt to understand what others think; to disagree, perhaps, but also to understand.

I've had discussions (simplified for the purposes of this book) that have gone much like this:

Friend: 'Do you agree with me or not, Susan?'

Me: 'Well, I agree with a lot of what you say, but I have some concerns and questions.'

Friend: 'Fine, but do you agree with me?'

Me: 'Sort of. But what about—?'

Friend: 'Well you're clearly not one of us then.'

The act of questioning, considering and challenging is surely a good thing. It's also entirely possible to really like a bit of something but not like the rest of it. Scooby and Scrappy Doo are the perfect, stupid example of this theory. I'm absolutely down with a dog solving crimes, but a talking nephew was a step too far. Things don't need to be so absolute.

Everything feels political now: what we eat, who we follow on Twitter, what we watch on television. While politics has always played a part in our lives, it seems to me that the blurring between what we believe and who we are has become the norm. When I was growing up we used to have dinner at six o'clock every evening just as Big Ben bonged on Radio 4 for the news. It would be on in the background as we ate, but then it was switched off and little consideration would be given to current affairs after that. The morning paper was read, the news was watched but in between there was, for many people at least, a period of calm. A time when no one was constantly updating an app, or checking opinion polls or mining our heads for data about what we think. Algorithms on Facebook know more about me than my family does, and they've certainly seen more photographs of me drunk. For reasons far too divergent and complicated to summarise in a sentence, recent political events have proven that for many what we believe is all that matters in deciding who we are. I'm more than happy to confess that I voted to remain in the European Union during the Brexit referendum. I like Europe. It has its faults but on balance I believe it better to stay in than leave. And more than that, no one appeared to be able to actually tell me what was going to happen if we left. Call me a cynic if you like but someone simply saying 'It'll be fine' didn't reassure me when I was about to have my tonsils removed, and it certainly didn't reassure me before Brexit.

Theresa May kept saying 'Brexit means Brexit', as if a tautologous definition was sufficient to satisfy curiosity. Maybe it's my traditional Scottish schooling but if I'd sat my Higher history exam and the question was 'What is the First World War?' and my answer was 'The First World War is the First World War' I'd have failed that exam. And rightly so. I appreciate, as do most people, that we can't know the unknowable, that we won't have all the answers to all of the questions, but it would be good to have some semblance of a plan.

The Brexit referendum seems to me a prime example of the tribal politics that plays such a part in our lives now. The animosity and lack of kindness that seem to be a feature of it make me feel like weeping at times. During that referendum, and indeed after it, I was confronted by people demanding to know how I voted.

Are you pro- or anti-Brexit? Tell me. Now. Tell me now and then I can judge you. And I will judge you. I don't care about any of your other views or why you voted the way that you did on this particular issue. I will also think that you're stupid if you voted the opposite way to me, because only I am correct on this issue.'

All I can say is that I'm a fairly ordinary (albeit fabulous) woman and I rarely vote or decide on any issue without having some sort of internal conflict. I entirely respect those who disagree with me as long as they can provide a reasoned argument. It seems to me that most people are centrist in approach and have leanings to the left or the right on some issues depending on personal circumstance. There are people who are hard left or hard right but the majority of us float in the middle and currents can blow us one way or the other.

All I really want from people is the kindness that comes with listening to a different point of view. To stop thinking that their viewpoint is the only one that matters. Challenging your own opinions is an essential part of discourse, but one that seems to have dropped out of fashion like snoods or pixie boots. I'm as guilty as anyone of becoming entrenched in my beliefs, but I know, from personal experience, that seeing both sides and examining what I believe, is crucial to accepting other viewpoints and to ultimately being kinder to everyone.

I'm a hugely opinionated person and one of the downsides of being so very sure of myself and what I think is that I have a pretty hard time admitting I'm wrong. I was convinced for years that the Elgin Marbles were just what they sounded like: a small collection of spherical toys probably unearthed in an old playground in Ancient Greece. Which Britain had probably stolen during the lunch break and refused to give back. Even when I was standing in the British Museum staring at a collection of classical Greek marble sculptures, inscriptions and architectural members that were originally part of the Parthenon and other buildings at the Acropolis, I demanded access to the real Elgin Marbles. Imagine my disappointment at seeing Cleopatra's Needle.

Sometimes when I get things wrong I do admit it, although an appropriate amount of time has to pass first. For example, I'm now prepared to admit, despite years of arguing otherwise, that Velma from *Scooby Doo* and Billie Jean King are not the same person.

There is a point in most young people's lives when they have to sit in a room with a careers officer and state their chosen profession. When I was younger I had very specific dreams. I wanted to be a Hollywood starlet, or a long-distance lorry driver, or a hit man. I still think I'd make a good hit person, certainly a better one than the people you see in films who play spies and assassins anyway. They're all far too attractive, far too noticeable. That's not to say I'm not attractive – I am in my own way. Indeed, after spending some time in my company you may well think, 'Oh, she's got a lovely face'. What I mean is that I'd be better than someone like Angelina Jolie, who by any measure is pretty uber-attractive. How could she fly under the radar? If you saw her you'd go, 'Look! There's Angelina Jolie! What's she doing in Morrisons at the fish counter?' As soon as the police started investigating a suspicious death the first thing you'd say is, 'Oh and I saw a really beautiful woman standing around with a gun.' Someone like me would be better in these films. I wouldn't be noticed. I'm sure that with very little effort I could easily look like the kind of woman who changes the sanitary bins at your local Wetherspoons. When was the last time you noticed her?

Sorry. I swerved off topic there, although in my defence I did warn you that might happen. So my careers officer asked me what I wanted to be when I grew up and even without asking I knew that 'lorry driver' and 'hit man' were not going to fly. I left school in 1992 and even in those relatively modern times I felt that the career options for girls were limited, if not by actual exam results then certainly by implication. We still had typing lessons for girls and it was very much assumed that we would all get married and have kids one day. I didn't want that, had reasonably good exam results, quite liked *Ally McBeal* and so said that I wanted to be a lawyer. I didn't really want to be a lawyer but sometimes you just need to say something in order to get out of an awkward meeting with a careers officer. So I went to Glasgow University without a clue what was about to happen but, as is the way of a Calman, bluffed my way through the first awkward months, and somewhat by accident, I settled in with a crowd of quite political types. It turned out I wasn't fashionable enough for the fashionable crowd, not sporty enough for the athletic group and not tall enough for the debating society (at least that's the reason they gave me. I didn't like to argue.). But the politicos and me would sit and argue philosophy and jurisprudence and navel-gaze until the sun came up. It was fun and simple. It was 1992 and, hard as it might be to remember, there was no Internet.

It was a golden age when people used to have what were called 'discussions', which didn't end after thirty seconds when someone looked up the 'answer' on their phone. These were the days when arguments would go on for weeks, months, years even. Saying it out loud now it sounds utterly ridiculous, but they were good times.

I hung out with the liberals, because I wanted to be one. I'd gone to quite a strict school and so I wanted everything in my life to be as liberal as possible. I wanted to drink, dance and cook naked (although I only ever tried cooking naked once. Spitting fat makes an interesting burn pattern, which can be difficult to explain). Of course, I didn't really know what a liberal was except that they seemed to be a lot more cheerful than those on the right wing of politics, whose party conferences always seemed to resemble a really badly attended wake at which no one really liked the deceased.

I was so desperate to fit in with the group that I listened to what they said, believed what they believed and took as gospel their points of view. I didn't so much *disagree* with what they were saying, I just didn't really *believe* a lot of it myself. But I hung in there and, in their company, I talked about everything from feminism to the concept of fraternity. From Karl Marx to Marks & Spencer.

Some of the most heated discussions we had surrounded the issue of capital punishment, a typical 'hot topic' of debate amongst those with too much time on their hands. (As an aside I must say that I always thought the phrase 'death penalty' rather understates the idea of killing someone. A penalty is something you get for speeding or for fare dodging, and the punishment for those things doesn't usually involve a priest and a last meal.)

Truth be told, I didn't know a lot about capital punishment. As far as I was concerned it had been abolished in the UK years before I was born and was a long-forgotten piece of history. But – and you now know how hard this is for me to say – I was wrong about that. It was only on 10 October 2003 that the UK acceded to the 13th Protocol of the European Convention on Human Rights, which prohibits the death penalty under all circumstances, meaning that the UK may no longer legislate to restore the death penalty while it is subject to the Convention. An interesting side note to remember as we face the yawning chasm of Brexit.

Our discussions were very much theoretical and abstract, however, and I enjoyed listening to the intellectual rough and tumble over a few pints about the pros and cons of capital punishment. One of the arguments for the death penalty is that the small chance of executing an innocent person is balanced out by the benefit to society of executing all the guilty ones. There are many counterarguments to that position, some of them very silly. You could suggest that the small chance of someone having their arms bitten off is balanced out by the benefit of having alligators in schools, so children can see wildlife up close. Or that the small chance that the little fish used in pedicures might acquire a taste for human flesh and evolve into a smaller, more voracious predator than the great white shark is balanced out by the benefit of people with more money than sense having nice-looking feet.

As with many other moral or ethical questions, there is a biblical argument, but it's hard to argue an eye for an eye is still relevant in today's society. There are many passages from the Bible that we would never consider validating now, and the selective process of taking guidance from the Bible to justify contemporary actions can be easily lampooned. Using punishments from history isn't really a good way to proceed, and many parts of the old 'justice' system have died out – appropriately so, because they're plain crazy! I've no doubt that if we looked to the past for justice in the here and now, I'd have been on the ducking stool years ago.

But our little group of liberal crusaders agreed that capital punishment was wrong and, with the arrogance that only a young person with no real experience of life could possess, I took the highest possible moral position and determined that the United States of America, a country that continued to use capital punishment, was wrong and stupid. My arrogance was so palpable it was like I was having a party for myself filled with balloons that had 'I know best' written on them.

One of the courses I chose to study at university, partly because it seemed less dull than boring Scottish law, concerned the American Supreme Court. If I'm being completely honest with you I also thought it would be quite easy. I'd watched a ton of John Grisham films, loads of *Law and Order* and of course *Cagney & Lacey*. Was there anything I didn't already know about American law? It also fed into my desire to be seen as a superhero for justice – Wonder Woman with a law degree, if you will.

And amongst my liberal friends it meant I could discuss, with an appropriate level of gravitas, the truth behind the theories. Or so I thought.

We started studying. I sat and listened to the key questions, the Supreme Court Judgments and the theories as to why capital punishment was constitutional. As I listened, I scoffed, because I knew it was wrong. Because I'd been told it was.

But one day I got the opportunity to challenge my own certainty and to think for myself. And for want of a more poetic way to put it, that day was the day I met a nun.

That in itself was a rather big deal, because it was the first time I'd met a real nun. I'd met lots of fake nuns in pubs and naturally I'd watched *The Sound of Music* every Christmas, but I'd never met a real nun before. It just so happened that the bona fide nun I encountered was a very special woman called Sister Helen Prejean, famously portrayed by Susan Sarandon in the Oscar-winning film *Dead Man Walking*. She came to talk to the American Supreme Court class about her campaign against the death penalty.

As she spoke about her personal experiences with prisoners on death row I had the sudden and rather stunning realisation that the nineteen-year-old me might not have all the answers. That my simplistic approach to the subject, perhaps purposefully, allowed me to ignore the complexity of the arguments. It was like a giant light bulb had come on over my head. I don't know if you ever get these moments, moments of great clarity like a doctor is shining a torch into your eyes to check your pupils. This was one of those moments, another, far earlier road to Damascus moment if you like, but with the added benefit of not having to actually walk anywhere. And as I listened to Sister Helen, the balloons at my party of arrogance began to deflate. She stood in front of us and calmly explained what capital punishment meant to her and what she had seen in the course of her work.

You might be wondering at this point why she'd even come to Glasgow, not widely considered to be the centre of the campaign against the death penalty. Quite simply, the Law School at the University of Glasgow ran a programme that allowed students to travel to America and to work with appellate projects in states that used capital punishment. One visit from Sister Helen was all I needed to persuade me that this was a mission meant only for me. Investigating crimes, perhaps finding the real murderer, changing lives. In my head I was a cross between Jodie Foster, Jessica Fletcher and Gandhi, but with a Scottish accent. Because, as my arrogance inflated again, that's what it'd be like. I'd seen *Silence of the Lambs*, that was all the research that was needed – right?

And so, with as much consideration as I might give to what socks I'd wear of a morning, I popped off to spend the summer in North Carolina: a white knight of justice, going to save America from itself. I was going to show the whole country how wrong they were.

I was nervous before I set off. For a start I hadn't travelled on my own any further from my home town than Glasgow (and my home town *was* Glasgow). To fly across the ocean without anyone to help me was, in truth, even more frightening than meeting prisoners on death row. I remember being told before I went that we shouldn't carry any information in our bags regarding our real purpose for visiting America in case we were refused entry at customs. The suggested tactic was to take books with us because that would help us look like 'normal' holiday-makers. The problem was I didn't have any books that weren't about law, and I wasn't exactly the most average of humans. How on earth was I meant to look normal? Luckily a friend of mine, one of the loveliest and most average (I mean that as a compliment) people I know, sat me down and gave me a tutorial on not being me. That might sound like a cruel and strange thing to do, but it wasn't. It was what I needed to get past security. And so with my nose piercing removed, my shaved head covered with as much hair as I could grow in a short period of time, my large second-hand army coat replaced with a borrowed Laura Ashley cardigan and a few Jackie Collins novels in my suitcase, I landed in the US of A. I sailed through customs with a smile. It turns out I *can* pretend to be just like everyone else when I try.

I landed at Raleigh–Durham airport and I found my way to the North Carolina Appellate Centre. My boss was dressed entirely in tie-dye, which he explained was down to his love of the Grateful Dead. He laughed, and I laughed, and I never told him I had no idea who the Grateful Dead were. I still don't.

The aim of the Appellate Centre was not to get prisoners released but instead to get their sentences commuted to life without parole. And it was with that clear mission statement that I threw myself into my work.

At the centre, I was assigned certain cases. 'Now we're getting down to business,' I thought. Getting to the heart of it: the investigating and the research. Our job was to review the cases, see if there were avenues for appeal on factual or legal grounds and then follow it up. This, I thought, was my moment.

We didn't just sit in the office either. In order to investigate one of my cases I was sent on a field trip to the Blue Ridge Mountains of Virginia. I never tired of singing that song although strangely many of the people who lived in the area seemed less pleased by my renditions. Myself and a psychologist called Al set off on a road trip to interview witnesses. It was like *Thelma and Louise* except I was in the car with a man, and we didn't drive off a cliff.

It sounds bizarre, but it *was* just like a film. We set off in the steaming summer sunshine and I was giddy with excitement. We arrived in a town high in the mountains where we were to interview a woman who had been a guard when one of my clients was in prison. We arranged to meet in the bar of a Holiday Inn at midday. It was clandestine, it was dangerous and it was exciting. And I can honestly say it's the only time I've been excited about being in a Holiday Inn. I wore a suit, because my mother had told me that was how you get taken seriously. I'd also brought some court shoes and, because I'd come from Scotland, some thick black tights. It was soon clear that a heavy pair of tights was a bad idea in the humidity of the mountains and my feet, unused to being constrained in a pair of court shoes, were so swollen they resembled sausages crammed into an ice-cube tray. Al and I sat in reception. I was ready for it. I was a people person. I had visions of interrogating the witness, of finding the missing piece of evidence in the case and of walking into the court like Atticus Finch to save a man's life. I had a list of detailed questions, which I was determined to drill out of the witness whether she liked it or not.

The witness arrived. She was a large woman whose build closely resembled that of a concrete traffic bollard. I could tell she wasn't happy because she was growling. I smiled. I tried to engage her in banter by asking her friendly questions about what it was like to live in such a pleasant town. She carried on growling. I carried on smiling. After about five minutes it was clear that things weren't going so well. I started to feel slightly unsure, but then dismissed it. I was from Glasgow, for goodness' sake. Nothing frightens a girl from Glasgow.

Then the most surprising thing happened. She beckoned me forward. I leaned towards her. I wondered if this was the moment where she would tell me the crucial piece of evidence I needed to save my client. She grasped my shoulder and quietly whispered in my ear, 'Just to let you know I've a loaded handgun under the table. And it's pointing at you.' I leaned back. I smiled again. I smiled for a very long time. Eventually I said, in an unnaturally high voice, 'Thank you very much for your time, it's been really useful. Goodbye.' I hobbled out as fast as my swollen little legs could carry me with Al trailing behind, oblivious as to what had just happened.

She did have a gun. As did the woman I interviewed at

a trailer park who produced a shotgun and started counting to ten. She didn't need to tell me what would happen when she got to ten; I could guess. And so I ran, quicker than Usain Bolt at the Olympics, as far away as I could. Twice in less than a week I'd had guns pointed at me.

I was confused. This wasn't what the theoretical discussion had prepared me for! And it got worse. As part of our work we had to read all of the files relating to our cases. We spoke to the victims' families to understand what effect the crimes had had. I saw pictures of the crime scenes, heard the tapes of 911 calls and, most astonishingly, I was confronted by the fact that one of my clients admitted that he'd committed the crime he was convicted of.

This was something I was completely unprepared for. I expected that I would be working to save innocent people. Those who had been unfairly convicted because of corruption or mistaken identity. But I'd never considered that someone might admit that they'd done it. But the man I'll call Simon had.

I wanted to meet this man. He'd messed with my safe, theoretical, arrogant opinions. I wanted to find out what he was like and whether or not I still believed what I thought I did. So I worked and worked and worked. I pushed for it. I said I was ready. I said I wouldn't be affected by it. I lied. And then one day my tie-dye-wearing boss called me into the office and said I could meet Simon.

I played it totally cool and asked my boss what he wanted me to achieve. I'd read in a book that you should always have outcomes to aim for, and it seemed an appropriate time to use that strategy. Except my boss told me

I was just to sit and have a chat, find out how he was. What? Not confront him? Not challenge him? Just have a chat?

But I got ready. I decided not to wear the court shoes and heavy tights this time. Truth be told I wasn't sure what an appropriate outfit was for a visit to a maximum-security prison, but after getting a shotgun pointed at me I was fairly certain that my outfit should be comfortable enough to allow me to run really fast at any time.

I stood outside the prison. A lot of things were running through my mind. But as I stood there, do you know the main thing that was causing me distress? Only the smallest and most ridiculous of details. You see I often watched *The X-Files,* which, if you haven't heard of it, is a tremendous science fiction television show starring Gillian Anderson. As I stood outside Central Prison in Raleigh I remembered that I'd watched a couple of episodes of the show that were allegedly set in the very prison that I was standing outside. But! The prison I was standing looking at bore no resemblance to the one on the television. *The X-Files* had lied to me! And even though it's a television programme about aliens I was disgusted by their lies. The truth wasn't out there at all.

Still stinging from the betrayal, I was probably less nervous than I should've been about what I was about to do. I walked into the jail. I had to present identification at the desk. I was asked to give up my firearm. I said I had no firearm; back home I'm still not trusted to carry scissors. And then I laughed. Then I quickly realised that making a joke was probably a bad idea. I was circled by a group of huge prison guards with belts overloaded with keys, torches and guns.

I was escorted through countless doors that clanged behind me. Oddly all I could think about was the opening credits of *Porridge*. As we walked through the corridors, which were painted a rather disturbing shade of green, I started to mumble, 'Norman Stanley Fletcher, you have pleaded guilty to the charges brought by this court, and it is now my duty to pass sentence.' Just imagine how unfunny *Porridge* would have been if Fletcher had been handed a death sentence in the opening titles. My enthusiasm started to diminish the deeper we got into the prison. It was like being desperate to attend a party only to find when you got there that the only people attending were your ex-partners. Everywhere I looked there were more doors, more guards, more guns. And then the last door opened.

I was shown into a room. It was small. A tatty old chair was screwed into the floor. I sat down and placed what notes I'd brought in front of me. A scratched and dirty screen of reinforced perspex separated the side I was on from the side where prisoners would sit. I sat and waited. As I did so it hit me what I was doing. I'd gone from sitting in a comfortable pub in the fancy West End of Glasgow, debating the theory of capital punishment, to a prison in North Carolina where I was about to meet someone who'd spent a decade on death row. The door opened, and Simon appeared. And what did I do? That's right, I smiled. I smiled at him because I had no idea what else to do. All my bravado, all my arrogance was gone. I was sitting in front of a man who knew that he would die soon unless someone like me found a way to stop that happening. We chatted for a while about the witnesses I'd spoken to and the way that the appeal was going. I knew what he'd done because I'd seen the files and spoken to the victims' families, but I wouldn't have *known* if I'd sat next to him in that pub in the West End of Glasgow. He didn't have anything written on his forehead. He didn't have glowing red eyes. He was just a man.

Eventually our short time together ended, and he left. I went back to the office. My boss asked me how he was and if I'd noticed anything odd at all. I said that the only thing that struck me as unusual was the fact that he never looked me in the eye, but I just assumed he was slumped forward because of the chains around his ankles. My Grateful Dead-loving mentor sat back and nodded wisely. Then he told me the truth. He said that my being sent to the prison was for a specific reason. It turns out that Simon only hurt one particular type of woman. Those with dark hair and dark eyes. Women who looked like his mother. Women who looked like me. They'd sent me in to see how he reacted. Which was pretty rude on their part. That's not really the way you should treat guests to your country, United States. It's as if they were saying, 'Oh, send the Scottish one, I'm sure she's expendable.'

So, my mentor had sent me into a room with someone who killed people who looked just like me. Possibly time to start looking for a new mentor?

That wasn't a light-bulb moment so much as a moment

when lights exploded in my head. That was when I realised that this is how you decide how you feel about something. By seeing it. By doing it. I'd spoken to relatives of victims; I'd spoken to those who'd perpetrated the crime. I'd argued till I was blue in the face, I'd been shouted at, I'd walked through demonstrations outside prisons and seen the looks of disgust on people's faces when I told them what I was there to do. I'd sat opposite a man who'd killed women who looked like me.

But I was there. I was finding out for myself. And what I found was that I agreed with my friends in Glasgow, but not because of a theoretical argument or a patronising viewpoint. Because I'd looked in the eyes of a guilty man who was going to die by the hands of the state. And I didn't want that to happen.

It was the first time in my life that I was truly scared, when I resolved to wear comfortable shoes so I could always run away, and I realised Gillian Anderson was a bloody liar.

It was also the first time in my life that I challenged my own beliefs. The naïve arrogance of youth meant I'd just assumed that everything I thought was right. I left North Carolina surer than ever that the death penalty was wrong, but I'd come to that conclusion on my own after seeing the evidence. However, even though I truly believe that we in Britain should never contemplate bringing it back, no matter the knee-jerk headlines or the right-wing politicians who clamour for the times when it was available, I don't stop talking to people who think it should be reintroduced. If I stopped speaking to people who I disagreed with then I would speak to literally no one. Not even my wife – we disagree about lots of things. I couldn't even rely on my cats, because they can't string a coherent sentence together.

While I can't go on a voyage of discovery about every issue, there is one thing I can do. Listen. I may disagree with a person's politics, but I like to think I could formulate an argument for *why* I disagree. I spoke to a very distinguished comedian about the art of political satire and we chatted for a while about TV shows and magazines that I'd enjoyed before I got into comedy myself. One of the things that sticks in my mind most of all is a show called *Spitting Image*, which was broadcast on British TV in the 1980s and 90s. While the quality may have varied, and the humour was often lost on me because I was too young to understand some of the stories, I remember clearly the impact that the sketches had on me. One in particular, which was broadcast on the eve of the 1987 general election, was a parody of the film *Cabaret* and featured latex puppets of Margaret Thatcher and her cabinet (it's on YouTube if you want to take a look at it). The sketch, which was written by a team determined to cast the Prime Minister in a deeply unflattering light as satire is wont to do, contains images including hospital wards shutting, the privatisation of the NHS and the increase in property prices. It's still a compelling piece of satire now and whilst it was clearly intended to shock, at its core it showed a genuine fear of what would happen to the country if the Conservative government were re-elected. My comedian friend told me that the reason why *Spitting Image* worked was because those writing it genuinely knew about the issues at hand. That they looked at the politicians on both sides and considered their characters. While many would disagree with the portrayal of individuals on the show, one of the reasons why the parodies hit home was that the writers were educated. I don't mean that they all had degrees, but they had an understanding of the substance of the issues they were parodying.

All this is not to say an opinion based on pure instinct is wrong. It can be just as valid as one provided by someone who has spent a lifetime researching and experimenting. But however one has arrived at their personal conclusion, it is still possible to listen to an opposing viewpoint and perhaps understand a little about why someone may disagree with you. It's those who refuse to consider that they may be wrong who cause the most harm, because they allow themselves to be ignorant of someone else's truth.

About ten years ago I was sitting backstage at a comedy club – this was in the early days of my career and I was far less sure of myself than I am now. One of the comics was discussing teaching and said, with absolute certainty, that he didn't understand the fuss about Section 28 because it didn't really harm anyone, did it? He addressed it to me as I was the only gay in the room and waited for my response. My view was, and remains, that it was harmful and was part of an overwhelmingly negative campaign about LGBTQ people in Britain. He, as a straight man who had never encountered a gay pupil, refused to accept my position. He had personally never met anyone who it had done damage to. I politely said that it very definitely affected me; this was dismissed with a sigh and a 'Well it would, wouldn't it, Susan?' Because I'm an over-emotional woman, you see. I'm a gay with a chip on my shoulder. I suggested that maybe he had had gay pupils and that they, perhaps, had felt less than confident about confessing how they felt because of the atmosphere surrounding the legislation. No matter how I tried to put the opposite viewpoint, he wouldn't listen. We parted ways with him feeling exactly the same as he always had and buying into the lie that everyone should just stop going on about it all.

It is possible to disagree with someone and still like them. It is possible that people may have a different view to yours but that their viewpoint is just as valid. To become entrenched and blind to differing viewpoints is isolationist and dangerous. Only by understanding differing viewpoints can we argue against them. I have, in my life, been persuaded to change my position on a number of political and moral issues. And it's entirely possible I will do so again.

My initial proposition was that political kindness could change the world and I still think it could. Kindness towards those with opposing ideas, kindness in expressing disagreement. Kindness in listening to others. Stopping the absolute declarations like 'All those who voted for Brexit are racist' and 'Everyone who voted to remain is a liberal snowflake traitor'. Human beings aren't absolute, and no issue is either. But all of this can only work if those who represent us behave appropriately. They need to take responsibility for how they behave, just as they expect us to.

You might disagree with my views on this and that's fine. In fact, if you do, then disagree away. Just do it with kindness, then you've illustrated my point exactly.

CHAPTER 5

TRAVELS WITH MY PLANT: STORIES OF KINDNESS FROM MY TOUR

IN the spring of 2017 I embarked on a stand-up tour of the country. It was my second major cross-country comedy jamboree and, as with my first attempt at entertaining the nation, I gigged in large towns and small hamlets to the many and the few. In fact, the only criteria when I tour are that the venue has to be accessible by train and have a Premier Inn nearby. A train station because my chronic fear of flying means I travel by locomotive wherever possible and a Premier Inn because they tend to be clean, have good Wi-Fi and fundamentally, you know what you're going to get. A Premier Inn won't surprise you with something unexpected, which is a bonus for me. The last thing I want after a long journey is to spend an hour trying to work out where the light switches are. And before you send me a terse tweet or email, no I'm not sponsored by said low-budget hotel chain. I have no financial ties to any company and there's no product placement in this book. Not that I'm against such things in principle. I'd have loved to write the sentence: 'I began writing this book by sitting at my desk and considering the world. I had to move my giant bejewelled Fabergé egg to get a better view, but then I could really get on with it.'

Contrary to what people might think when they look at a hugely successful (ha!) comedian such as myself, I don't have an extensive entourage, or a tour bus, or even a manager who accompanies me on my travels. Instead I have a rucksack, a sturdy suitcase and train tickets to the farthest reaches of the UK. While it undoubtedly gets lonely at times, it does give me a lot of freedom. I arrive at venues and greet the staff, set up the extensive on-stage decorations (one table, one microphone stand, one bottle of water) and after the show I'll often scuttle through the lobby of a theatre or arts centre (because it's the only exit available) and, whether I like it or not, hang out with the audience.

Truth be told, I like that connection with people who come to see my shows. They're generally lovely folks who just want to chat about my stories or tell me how much they like Radio 4 or cats, and I've spent many an enjoyable evening in the company of complete strangers, chatting about all sorts of nonsense. They're also, in my experience, a pretty diverse group of people. Because I do so many things I get a wide range of people attending my shows, which makes for a lovely diagram:

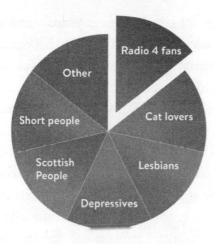

I like the diversity. It's wonderful to see a group of people who otherwise would have no reason to spend an evening together, sitting in the darkness listening to my nonsense. It's also a challenging environment for stand-up. If the audience knows me from a light-hearted entertainment show they may be surprised by some of my material, which can, on occasion, be rather forceful. And those who come expecting a political diatribe can be confused by my ten-minute routine on how much I love Jane McDonald from *Cruising with Jane McDonald*. I do love her by the way. In my dining room I have a collection of all my prized possessions that comprises the *Strictly* glitterball for winning the tour, my *Pointless Celebrities* trophy and a signed photo of Jane McDonald. On it she wrote 'Sorry I missed you'. One day I'll meet her, one fine day.

The most exciting part of stand-up, as opposed to radio and television work, is that the audience are right there in front of me and feedback is instant and unavoidable.

It's much more of a dialogue than something that's recorded and edited before broadcast. A live audience can tell me exactly what they think of me, but I can also ask them their opinions and thoughts. Before I started touring the show I knew I was going to be writing this book and realised that I would have access to thousands of brains by way of a captive audience of guinea pigs. I was acutely aware of the fact that while I have my own opinion of what kindness is, it might differ vastly from other people's. In order to have a broad range of views, I asked my audiences to tweet me in the interval of the show and let me know the kindest thing that anyone had ever done for them. I gave them no further guidance other than to say that no act was too small or too big, too silly or too serious. I also didn't define what kindness was because I wanted to leave the interpretation entirely up to them. The responses were varied, beautiful, funny and, on some occasions, rather emotional. There were far too many to include them all, so instead I've selected a few and given my own thoughts on them and the places in which they were collected.

The one thing that ties all these episodes together, of course, is that people have remembered them. That inter-action with a friend or stranger affected them so much that they felt moved to share it with me. That's a big deal, and if nothing else it proves that a small act of kindness can make a big difference to someone.

Before we begin this part of the journey I'd like to clarify why I've called this chapter and all subsequent groupings of audience feedback 'Travels with my Plant'.

It's partly because, quite simply, Plant rhymes with Aunt and it made me laugh. But also because I enjoy the visual image of tiny me, with a Yucca plant strapped to my back, attempting to get on a busy commuter train from Cheltenham to Cardiff. I did that journey once. The Yucca plant wouldn't have survived.

Keswick

Keswick, a town nestled in the Lake District, is a really lovely place, the audiences always warm and engaging and honest. Different areas of the UK produced vastly varying numbers of tweets; in fact, in some places there were distressingly few tales of kindness. Not in Keswick. I got an avalanche of joy from them. The first story I've picked involves wildlife (always guaranteed to get my attention) and I've condensed the numerous tweets into one story.

Bekki @Bex701
Mum got a knock on the door – it was the postman there to tell her that a hedgehog had just hidden under her car. On explaining that she had to go to work soon, the postie put his bag down and attempted to retrieve the hedgehog. Meanwhile next-door neighbour came out with big stick to help. Mum went to get ready for work. When she came down, there was a 'sorry we missed you' note with the news that the hedgehog had been successfully evacuated to new home! Teamwork!

This story appeals to me on a very basic level. A bunch
of strangers working together to save a hedgehog who
may neither know nor care what's happened, depending
on your views of the sentient nature of animals (I think
they know everything that's happening, personally). Firstly,
there was the postman, who had a job to do but spotted
a lost animal under a car and cared enough to tell someone;
and then there was the neighbour, who saw what was
happening; and then the final denouement of the note
through the door. A tiny short story, which Bekki's mother
remembered and recounted. Gorgeous.

Nichola Rae @RaeN_84
A man saw me struggling to push my husband's wheel-
chair up North Bank St, Edinburgh – so offered to take
him to the top for me.

Kindness in a different form here. I've always believed
that Edinburgh shouldn't have spent all that money on
installing a tram system and instead should have installed
escalators everywhere. It's a curious place where absolutely
everything feels like it's uphill. It's easy to think that it's
a small thing to help someone out, but it sometimes feels
like a big thing to take the step to ask. Should I say something, should I step in, are they OK, will they be annoyed
at me? I always think that I'd rather ask if someone needs
help than spend the rest of the day worrying if they're
OK. When I travel in London, especially on the incredibly
busy Tube, I'm always heartened to see strong young people
helping with prams and suitcases, and it angers me a little

when they don't. On a recent train from Glasgow to London I saw an older couple who appeared to be on their holidays because of the bags they carefully arranged around their seats. As the train approached the station I got up, grabbed my bag and waited to see what happened. Nothing was the answer. No one offered to help them or checked to see if they were OK. My fellow passengers just went about their business because they were the most important and busy people in the world. I casually asked the couple if they needed me to help with their cases, as it was quite a step down to the platform. They smiled, said yes, I lifted them down, they said thank you and we went our separate ways. It took thirty seconds.

Sarah
A little act of kindness – I gave a pound to a woman in a car park, as she didn't have enough money.

This is an act of kindness that's dying out. Not because of the disintegration of the moral fabric of society, but because of the introduction of the Automatic Number Plate Recognition car park. Soon we won't be able to give people a free hour of parking. So, do it while you can.

Inverness

If you haven't been to Inverness, you should go. It's gorgeous and I was inundated with fantastic tales of joy. One of them stuck with me long after the show was over.

Eilidh Little @LittleEilidh
Kindness; when behind a woman in the co-op short of cash for her shopping my wife said 'here's that fiver I owe you'.

Kindness doesn't simply exist in the gesture itself, of giving five pounds to someone who needs the money, it's in the way that it's done. Considering the feelings of the person involved, the potential embarrassment that they might feel being short of cash and the delightfully offhand way that the conversation took place. This remains one of my favourite acts of kindness, mostly because it seems so instinctive and generous.

CHAPTER 6
BODY CONFIDENCE
HOW TO TAKE YOUR
CLOTHES OFF WITHOUT
HATING YOURSELF

PEOPLE sometimes ask whether being on a show like *Strictly* changed me. And the answer is yes. Absolutely it did. But not just the bit where I learned to dance and finally realised what a scatter chassé was. The biggest change was me. Every Saturday night I stood in my dressing room at Elstree Studios, looking in the mirror at a woman who bore no resemblance to the one I'd been looking at for the past four decades. I needed to look at myself because 11 million people were about to do the same. And this act of self-reflection forced me to start dealing with the one issue that I've been avoiding all my life. Putting it simply, and somewhat harshly, I can't stand the way I look. I really can't. Sometimes that's difficult for people to understand or even believe because what they see is a confident woman, striding out on stage and taking no prisoners. But that's an act. That's what I do to cope. On the *Strictly* live tour I would often say how much the show had helped my self-confidence and I could hear people laughing in the audience. They weren't being cruel;

I think they thought I was telling a joke because how on earth could that be true? Surely I was being a typical self-deprecating comedian? I really wish I was. Sadly, the truth was exactly as I told it.

Much of this book is about kindness and joy as an abstract and broad concept. As I sit in my study looking out at the city of Glasgow, many of the ruminations in my book concern the world and how we can help in a global and a general way to make things better. Big-picture thinking, blue-sky theories, running things up the flagpole as they say. But kindness doesn't always need to be expressed to others; in fact being kind to ourselves can have the knock-on effect of increased positivity all round. But being nicer to the person we see in the mirror every day can, in many ways, be the most difficult act of all. It can be easier to have empathy for a stranger than cut yourself some slack for having some cheesecake on a rainy Tuesday evening in November.

I am not good at being kind to myself – quite the opposite. I would say that I was a complete and utter failure who should give up trying because I'll never be any good. See? I'm my own harshest critic in every way. During my worst times I don't know why anyone would ever bother spending a single moment with me. Regarding my looks, in base terms I think I'm the fattest, ugliest, most horrific-looking woman in the world. You may think that I'm exaggerating my own self-hatred but I'm most certainly not. When *Strictly* started I clearly remember the shock expressed by my fellow competitors when they asked if I'd watched the show back and I would, with the usual Calman vigour, shout, 'Of course not! I'd be sick on myself.'

It's easier to use someone else's words to express how I feel about me, and the closest I've found is the writer William Mearns, who wrote the poem 'Antigonish' in 1899. The first verse reads:

> As I was going up the stair
> I met a man who wasn't there!
> He wasn't there again today,
> Oh how I wish he'd go away!

I think of myself as intermittently invisible, appearing for a time and then gone again. Deliberately disappearing but somehow still about. It's a tactic of self-preservation I've employed for years in order to deal with my own opinions of myself. From the very start of my comedy career I could never watch anything that I appeared on. If I accidentally caught sight of myself on the television and wasn't allowed to switch it off (for some reason my wife enjoys seeing what I've been doing with my time) I would hide behind the sofa until it was all over, much like I did when I was a child and the Daleks appeared on *Doctor Who*. Indeed, I wouldn't even listen to myself on the radio because the sound of my own voice made me feel nauseous. I would take part in a show and then forget all about it. What's done is done and I don't need to see the awful evidence of my own fat face staring back at me in my own living room. People often express disbelief when I confess this opinion of myself. It's so utterly harsh that it sounds like something a troll on the Internet would spout forth, but it's been a long-held belief of mine that I am, quite honestly, repulsive. The reasons for my lack of self-confidence are complex and I have done a huge amount of work through therapy to try to dispel some of my harshest self-criticisms. But that opinion always lurks, like a single sock in the bottom of the laundry basket. It should really be thrown away, you try to get rid of it, but somehow it always pops back up again.

This self-pitying nonsense is all well and good and I carried on quite unhappily in this state of mind for many years. I have little doubt that if I hadn't jumped into the world of dancing I would have carried on being miserable and wallowing in self-loathing. The thing is, there's one environment where a one-woman pity party is tough to sustain, and that's *Strictly Come Dancing*. Having body confidence issues when 11 million people are about to see your pants as you twirl isn't workable. Trying to hide away when you're on the biggest show on television is as easy as avoiding hearing Mariah Carey's 'All I Want for Christmas Is You' from November onwards.

Why did I do it then; why did I agree to be the most visible I'd ever been if I hated myself so much? I'd been watching the show for years; I knew that the ladies wore short dresses and that 'sexy' was part of the deal. I may hate the way I look but I know I'm not stupid – surely if I found myself and the way I looked so appalling I should simply have hidden away in my living room for the next decade. The answer to this puzzling change of direction is simple. Sometimes I do things and I have no idea why.

I'm the most risk-averse woman on the planet and yet fifteen years ago I gave up a highly paid job in corporate law that I'd studied and trained for years to get in order to earn no money as a comedian. Why? No idea. Genuinely. I'd always wanted to be a stand-up but then I've wanted to do a lot of things with my life. Why I decided that this was the time to suddenly find the courage to do what I wanted to with my life I have no idea. My only answer is that sometimes I get an urge to jump. Like when you're at the top of a building and you look over the edge and you wonder if you stepped off if you could fly. Sometimes, about every fifteen years or so, I do the exact opposite of what I think I should do. Just to see what happens. I look forward to my mid-fifties when I decide it would be a brilliant idea to become a rodeo clown.

Thus, despite having no self-confidence, despite never having danced before, despite feeling sick at the thought of wearing a dress, I said yes to the show. I dealt with all of my fears by doing what I do best: ignoring them completely. Perhaps, just perhaps, I would be the first contestant who would be allowed to wear jeans – or better still, pyjamas – on the show. In moments of sanity the sensible part of me knew that wasn't going to happen and I steeled myself for what was to come. How could I get through this period of my life without ever actually confronting myself at any time? My tactic was simply to not look at myself, or any photo taken of me for the length of time that I was in *Strictly*. Easy. Then I wouldn't have to confront the terrible truth of how I looked; I could go back to my life and pretend nothing had ever happened.

I was pretty pleased with myself as this plan seemed fool-proof, and so I embarked on the *Strictly* journey with metaphorical blinkers strapped to my face.

I've never had to pluck up as much courage in my life as the first day I went to the studios and for my initial meeting with the wardrobe department. Imagine the scariest thing you've ever had to do and multiply that fear by infinity. I'm terrified of sharks but at that moment, just before I had my appointment, I would rather have jumped into a swimming pool full of great whites than have anyone ask me about fashion.

Here's how it went: I walked into a room. Four lovely women were waiting for me with a rack of dresses that could have come off the set of a Carmen Miranda movie. I'm in jeans, trainers and a T-shirt. I'm wearing my best bra, which is only two years old. Maybe three. The elastic had certainly gone. I eyed the team suspiciously; I could see them slowly drawing breath. Behind them was a rack of shoes containing terrifying heels, as if someone had placed a perfectly good shoe on a huge nail and said, 'Go on then, wear that.'

I realised that I should strip off, because it's difficult to try on skin-tight dresses over clothes; luckily, I was wearing my best pants (only one year old). My rational mind said that the team had seen many, many semi-naked people through the years and I was only one of hundreds of terrified people they'd dressed. Besides, no one would be judging me. Well, apart from me. I would definitely be judging me. I stood in my pants, trying to make it seem like I was totally OK with everything as three of the four women physically wrestled me into a dress. If you've ever watched the process of making a sausage, where several pounds of meat are stuffed into a narrow casing, that was me. But we tried on dresses and I was asked what I did and didn't want to wear. I said I wasn't very keen on dresses in general, so they rephrased the question. 'What parts of your body are you uncomfortable with?' I made a broad sweeping gesture from under my nose to my ankles. Undoubtedly if they'd had a bottle of gin they would have started drinking there and then. Let me say up front, by the way, that the wardrobe team were extraordinary: every single person only wanted us to feel comfortable and happy and never made us wear anything that we didn't want to. But when all you want to do is dress like Bridget Jones on a night in, it's something of a problem.

But we battled through, tried on frocks and sequins and I was very brave. They were kind and understanding and wonderful. But it became alarmingly clear to me that this was just the beginning. This was simply the first fitting of hundreds that would come afterwards for the many outfits I'd be required to wear. And I was in a small room at Elstree Studios, so no one could see me. At some point I was going to have to wear things like this in public, on television. I needed to go all in or go home. And I hadn't bought a return train ticket. Was I prepared to jump off the cliff and let *Strictly* consume me, or would I put my pyjamas back on and retreat to my comfort zone?

In *Cheer Up Love* I wrote extensively about my appearance, and my conclusion at the time was that I was happy wearing waistcoats and jackets – dressing, as I put it, like a miniature Marlene Dietrich. And I was. And I am. But my comfort in the way I dressed didn't necessarily stem from a positive place. I was always afraid of changing the way I looked because staying in a safe zone meant that I knew what I was, and no one could laugh at me. If I dressed in a particular and slightly eccentric style I could own it, I could cover up the bits I hated and pretend to the world that I was happy with who I was. I was wearing a costume of tweed and pinstripes to protect myself. Could I face doing the same with sequins and glitter?

The most difficult part of the whole show was this inner struggle with how I looked – putting myself out there in a new way with no waistcoast to protect me or bow tie to wiggle. It was, without question, the greatest challenge of my life. And I know that people might wince when I write things like that. What kind of challenge is it to wear a skirt when every day people are fighting real battles, facing off against violence and intimidation, attempting to feed their children and simply survive? I don't equate my attempts to cha-cha-cha with others' very real struggles but for me, and my head, this was the most difficult thing I'd ever done.

It didn't help that before the show had even started I received a fair amount of criticism from some parts of social media and the press because of what I'd written in *Cheer Up Love*. That because I'd said I was happy not being all girly, I was somehow betraying myself and others and 'selling out'. Indeed, some people said that I was complying with 'hetero-normality', and that by wearing a dress and make-up I was in some way losing my lesbian identity. It was a curious storm to be at the centre of. I'd assumed that the LGBTQ community would be pleased that a gay woman, who was comfortable with who she was, who was supported by her family and was political in her campaigning for equality, was appearing on the biggest entertainment show on television. I wasn't prepared for the negativity and the criticism. One of the greatest changes that have taken place for my community in the past couple of decades is that, hopefully, the stereotypes about gay people have evaporated. Some people might still believe that lesbians are all butch, man-hating dykes but hopefully those people are few and far between. It's a silly thing to have to say, but lesbians are people. And people are all very different from each other. In the same way as I find it offensive to be labelled a 'female' comedian, I find it odd that being a 'lesbian' means that I have to comply with a set of rules of which I have no knowledge.

Lesbians can dance with men. Some don't want to and that's grand. Lesbians can wear dresses and make-up. Some don't want to and that's brilliant. For one part of a community to insist that others comply with their opinions of what we should be is as restrictive as the stereotypes that the heterosexual community have for many years applied to us. And besides, doing a bit of dancing didn't mean that I had lost my political edge. But for me, Tess and Claudia casually chatting about my wife on television was fantastic. A woman tweeted me to tell me of a conversation that had happened in her living room on a Saturday night when *Strictly* was on. She was sitting on the sofa with her mother on one side and her young daughter on the other. Three generations of one family glued to the box. After I'd been on and my wife had appeared (as she always did) supporting me, her mother had remarked, 'Susan Calman has a wife?' in a questioning tone. Her daughter (who was around eight years old) apparently said, in a matter of fact way, 'Of course she has. Women can marry other women, you know.' The woman's mother nodded, and everyone went about their business. Because women can marry other women, and they can also make their own decisions about television shows they want to appear on.

For me it was quite simple. I wanted to be on *Strictly*. I wanted to dance. And yes, part of me did want to wear dresses like I'd seen countless other women wear. I'd just never had the courage to do it before. I also think that one of the greatest things about humanity is our capacity to change and grow. Confronting my fears about who I was and how I looked was, in my view, a good thing. Because if I could do it, then anyone could. In the same way that I wanted to write about depression to make people realise that it wasn't just doom and gloom, I was determined to show the great British public that you didn't need to be twenty years old and stick thin to dance on television. If I could get over my self-hatred, then maybe other people watching could get some confidence and change their lives too.

And so it began. The most important thing to realise, especially if you don't know much about me, is that I am exceptionally good at pretending I'm fine. I'm brilliant at looking confident when I don't actually feel it. And so, in many ways this was a simple thing for me to do. I've performed stand-up shows when feeling utterly horrific and an audience would never know. But this was different. Because I knew that I was exposing myself (not literally) to about 11 million people, most of whom had no idea who I was. The relative anonymity when I started made things slightly easier as there was very little pressure on me, but also more difficult because I felt I had to prove myself very quickly or I'd be voted out.

The discussion with the wardrobe department had established a few basics: I didn't want to wear anything too short or too low cut or that exposed my arms. I've inherited my family arms, which are not the most lovely of things, and the last thing I wanted was for my graceful moves to be interrupted when my bingo wings smacked me in the face. Luckily, as I mentioned, they responded immensely kindly, and from the very beginning of my time on the show I felt cared for and supported and loved by the terrifying women with the sewing needles.

Then there were the shoes. I have a feeling they knew what they were up against when they offered me a pair of ladies' Latin shoes with a four-inch heel. I put them on and started to hyperventilate. The air was far too thin up there. On the plus side though I did finally find out what it felt like to be over 5 foot tall (I didn't like it, although it would make shopping at the supermarket a bit easier). I literally have never worn a pair of heels like that – in fact the last time I wore anything resembling a pair of lady shoes was way back at the school dance where I think I was forced into a pair of slightly raised Clarks shoes in an attempt to make the Laura Ashley dress my mum had bought me look in some way attractive.

I was aware of the fact that I was trying to learn a new skill (dancing) while learning another new skill (walking). On the third occasion where I nearly killed myself by simply changing direction, a decision was made. I would wear what was kindly referred to as 'young adult' ballroom shoes. Size two and a half. But more importantly they had two-inch heels, which meant that there was less of a danger of me dying on national television. It wasn't ideal, and I could see the pain in the producers' eyes as some of the other celebrities twirled away in monstrous towering creations while I clumped along like I was off to the shops on a Saturday morning. I was nothing if not a challenge. To everyone.

The first time I stepped out for the launch show, in a dress and heels and big hair and glitter and sparkles, it was without question an out-of-body experience. I honestly don't remember a great deal of that day apart from really hoping I didn't fall over. I muttered to myself, 'Don't embarrass yourself, Calman,' and set off down the red carpet. The only experience I can equate it to is when I had my tonsils out at the age of twenty-one. I'd never had an operation before and it turns out I'm allergic to morphine, codeine and anything else fun that dulls pain. I ended up in a bit of a trance state without any comprehension of what was happening. That's what the launch show of *Strictly* was like. I would occasionally catch a glimpse of myself in a mirror and wonder why Elizabeth Taylor was looking back at me.

My fellow contestants all seemed so at ease with themselves. They were glamorous and beautiful, and I was standing at the edge like I'd sneaked into a wedding photograph. The most I remember of that day is the incredible pain the shoes caused. I may have small feet but they're as wide as the Nile, and when I finally peeled them off at the end of the day the marks of the straps were etched into my feet. Red welts that marked the beginning of my dancing career.

After the excitement of the launch show it was down to business, the dancing and more outfits. Week one was fine – a Viennese waltz meant I was wearing a beautiful 50s-inspired dress that I felt almost comfortable in. The shoes still caused me problems though. I was in ballrooms with very little give and no padding on the sole, which, for someone used to wearing trainers, caused the tendons in my feet to seize up on a regular basis. One of the most common events in the rehearsal room with Kevin was the sight of him nervously scratching his head and quietly saying, 'Shall we try it with the shoes? I mean only if you want to.' I would then throw my trainers at the wall, put on my ballrooms and hobble around screaming, 'IS THIS WHAT YOU WANT? DO I LOOK LIKE A LADY NOW?'

Week two was a Charleston, a dance I'd been really looking forward to. I love the 1920s and 30s and I couldn't wait to get stuck in. The dress was short admittedly, but it fitted the style. I had a wig and a pair of flat shoes! FLAT SHOES! Oh, the joy of dancing without heels – I ran around, jumped off things and felt like me again.

I was keeping it together. I could do this; I still wasn't looking at myself in the mirror, but I could do it. Then week 3 happened and everything started to crumble. Week 3 is movie week in *Strictly* and it's a huge deal. Not only is it a milestone but it's also when the big costumes and special effects are wheeled out and you get to let loose creatively. Kevin and I had spent a great deal of time talking about what we could do because I really wanted to do something very different from anything that had been done before. The problem is that very few fun films have women at the centre of them. When choreographing a dance, Kevin wanted to make sure that whoever I was playing was the star of the film concerned. There's no point in bringing a film to life if the female character isn't important. (As a side note, this was one of the most wonderful moments of my relationship with Kevin. While he was teaching me how to dance, I was teaching him about the Bechdel test. If you don't know what that is, it's a simple test about fiction or films that names the following three criteria: (1) it has to have at least two women in it, who (2) talk to each other, about (3) something besides a man. Try it next time you watch a movie or a TV show. It's enlightening. My darling Kevin embraced this new approach to entertainment like the gent he is.)

After making him listen to a short lecture on feminism, I put forward a number of suggestions to Kevin. I was sure that these films and characters would work and that they were entirely different from anything anyone had seen before:

1. My favourite – Hannibal Lecter and Clarice Starling. Supposedly this wasn't family friendly enough. I disagree. It shows how two very different people can get along despite a number of obstacles. These are lessons children should learn. I also thought the idea of Kevin being wheeled out on a trolley would be fun. Apparently, I 'take things too far'.

2. Jaws and Michael Caine from the classic film *Jaws 4*. I would be the shark, Kevin would be Michael Caine. I always like to surprise an audience and what better way to do this than remaking one of the worst shark movies of all time as an American smooth? Apparently, the fin would make lifts difficult.

3. Ripley and the Alien. See number 1.

4. The Queen and Tony Blair from the film *The Queen*.

5. *Fatal Attraction*. Enough said.

My ideas were, unfairly in my view, dismissed out of hand and Kevin suggested that we come up with something that might be more appropriate. A fairly intense brainstorming session followed, fuelled by numerous cups of tea and biscuits. What became absolutely clear was that there isn't a lot of choice for women when it comes to strong role models. And most of them had been done before. Suddenly I had a moment of inspiration. I'm a huge comic-book fan, as is my dance boyfriend, and both of us, at almost the same time, looked up and said the magical words 'Wonder Woman'. Perfect! The new film with Gal Gadot had been released and she was amazing in it. Kick-ass, beautiful, strong and everything a tiny Calman wants to be.

We pitched it and were told that were we to get through to week 3 I could be Wonder Woman. I had my customary Friday meeting with the wardrobe department, who showed me their initial plans for the costume. They work a week in advance for all the dancers, so they get a head start on what we're all going to wear to get a fair idea of where the designs are going. To my shock I wasn't wearing leather armour like Gal Gadot; instead I would be wearing the 1970s Linda Carter outfit. (For those of you who like rules, you should know that they made a movie out of the Linda Carter series, so we weren't cheating in movie week.)

I completely understood the reasoning. The 70s outfit is the most recognisable incarnation of Wonder Woman; it's also colourful and can be blinged up in the way that *Strictly* costumes are. But I was worried. Would people laugh at me? A short, fat lesbian from Scotland trying to be Wonder Woman? And not just Wonder Woman – THE Wonder Woman, the one who all of us remember and love. To top it all off my dance that week was a samba. I'd always known that in the spectrum of possible dances anything that required hip movement or rhythm would be tough. I could just about muddle through some ballroom by looking haughty but Latin dances? I am not a hot lady with fast-moving legs. I am a tepid lady who likes to take her time.

We got to rehearsing in Glasgow, Kevin gently shoving me in the right direction and politely suggesting that I needed a little bit more bounce than I had. The steps were tough but the difficulty of doing a botafogo was nothing compared to the first time I tried on the costume. It was beautiful, it was flattering, it was amazing, but it was so far outside my comfort zone that I completely froze. I remember crying to my wife the night before the show, sobbing that I was going to make a fool of myself in front of the nation. She tried her best to make me feel better, but it didn't work. Right up to the point that the show was about to start I was in bits. Everyone was supportive and lovely, but I felt like a fat blob in a sweetie wrapper.

Just before we climbed up the stairs for our entrance, Kevin took me by the shoulders and said, 'You are a strong powerful woman. You're Beyoncé, Gal Gadot, Michelle Obama, Helen Mirren, Gillian Anderson, Shonda Rhimes, Lady Gaga. Now go out there and strut like you believe it.' I knew that I had to do something. I had to make this work and I knew that at home there were thousands of women and girls who felt the same way that I did about themselves. I was going to do it for them. And so I did. I strutted and I snapped my fingers and I was a strong woman in charge of the world. And yes, some people I'm sure found it funny, but many people had the opposite reaction. To my surprise I was inundated with emails and tweets from people saying that they found it empowering. If I could be Wonder Woman, then anyone could. I was standing at Euston station the morning after the show waiting for the train home and a random stranger stood in front of me and did the Wonder Woman crossed-arms salute. Then two small children ran up and did the same. The ticket collector on the train shook my hand. On the *Strictly* tour the reaction to the Wonder Woman dance was incredible and I always said the same thing to the audience. That anyone can be Wonder Woman, because I didn't think I could and there I was.

More than 11 million people in Britain and many more around the world would watch us dance every week. It's difficult to sustain my usual level of self-hatred while being exposed to so many people so I had to, slowly, learn to be kinder to me. To let myself enjoy what was happening. I know I'm not alone in suffering from low self-confidence and that for a lot of people their harshest critic is the voice in their own head. But, for me at least, that feeling of negativity then feeds into other aspects of my life. If I leave the house in the morning hating myself, heaven help anyone I meet.

It's not easy to change the habits of a lifetime so I'll simply tell you what I did. Before I started on the show I never looked in a mirror. Ever. I would put on clean clothes, run my fingers through my hair and hope that what I was wearing didn't look too frightful. This was particularly difficult in my old flat. We bought it cheap because it hadn't been decorated in decades and the previous occupants had extensively renovated the property by ripping out all the original, and beautiful, features and replacing them with everything that was fashionable in the 1970s. Cork tiles, ceilings lowered by sheets of plywood, built-in cabin beds. But there was a special level of hell reserved for the bathroom. That was something quite spectacular.

It's difficult to adequately describe the true horror of the room. As you entered, one wall was entirely covered with mirrored tiles. Consequently, there hadn't been a single night since I'd moved in where I hadn't screamed thinking someone else was in the bathroom with me. The rest of the room was clad in pine – badly fitted, naturally – with the obligatory cork tiles on the floor and a solitary, homemade, shower cubicle with a light suspended by a piece of string (I know, how desperately safe). It was half Swedish porn set, half serial killer lair. A room of mirrors had to be negotiated carefully and mostly with eyes closed, as I just couldn't stand looking at myself.

I could function like that because I could sort of guess how I looked. Unfortunately, it's a bit more difficult to guess how you look when dancing. In my head I was pretty sure that I was as elegant as Darcey Bussell (sorry Darcey) but wishing and hoping wasn't going to get me through. I had to watch myself dance, at least in rehearsals, to check that the footwork was correct. My dance boyfriend Kevin used to film us practising so that he could run through what I was doing wrong and he found it quite curious that I refused to watch myself back. I think in the first week he thought I was being precious and, despite my lack of dance experience, considered myself above criticism. Far from it.

I realised quite quickly that I had to get on board and I had to watch the recordings, but I would studiously only glance at the bottom half of the screen. As time went on and I became more comfortable with this process, I sort of ignored myself and instead simply looked at the technique. I would allow myself to perhaps see what my arms were doing and then my face. I didn't ever get to the stage where I enjoyed the experience, but I did start to feel slightly less harsh than I had before. For example, my legs haven't seen the light of day since I last played hockey in approximately 1992, but I have to say that my sturdy calves aren't horrific. They're actually all right. Also, the make-up and hair magicians often made me look quite nice. Sometimes I even – and I hesitate to write this – quite liked how I looked. I started to walk with a bit more confidence, I held my head higher and I began to feel better about myself. And I started to be kinder to myself in other ways. Yes, I wasn't the best dancer, but I was OK. I may not have had all the moves, but I gave it my best and no one could accuse me of not trying. I realised that when I stopped hating myself and began being kinder it felt really lovely.

The process of getting to that stage in quite a short period of time was detailed. What I tried to do was pick something small; I figured that if I went all out for internal kindness straight off the bat I'd probably fail. You can't suddenly change the way you feel about yourself otherwise we'd all have done it years before, right? So, I looked at small bits of me, both physically and mentally, and tried to flip them from negative to positive. No, I'm not graceful. I'm short and stocky. But you know what that makes me? Powerful. I was able to quickstep faster than Usain Bolt. I have a low centre of gravity, so I was excellent at the jive kicks. I wasn't the skinniest, but I could entertain and hopefully convey the story of the dance through the television to the people at home. The most useful quote that I always returned to during the show was from Maya Angelou:

'I've learned that people will forget what you said, people will forget what you did, but people will never forget how you made them feel.'

This is not a boastful statement – I hate arrogance in every way – but Kevin (mostly Kevin) and I did make people feel something. I had to be kind to myself by allowing myself to acknowledge that. If nothing else, people could feel the joy that we felt when we danced radiating out of their television screens.

I know we made people feel something because of the way they reacted, and still react, when I meet them. People smile. And a huge number of those who I encounter want to hug me. I can't tell you how many times I've been in the queue at the supermarket only to find myself enveloped in a stranger's arms. Last week I went to my local pub and exited a toilet cubicle only to be enveloped by an enthusiastic woman who simply wanted to tell me that she loved me on *Strictly*. I don't mind that, by the way. Unless I'm holding eggs, or I've not done my belt up properly. Then it just looks a bit suspicious. I don't know why people want to wrap their arms around me, but they do. And I let them. Because they want to show me how they feel.

Susan Calman

In my experience it's easier to be kind to others when you feel it towards yourself. Constantly being angry at who you are or depressed about the way that you look is tough. Looking at myself in the mirror is still an uncomfortable experience and I don't enjoy it, but I do make myself do it. I look in the mirror and say, 'You're not ugly, you're not hideous, you're an OK person.' It works.

Because of *Strictly*, for the first time in my life I was being kind to myself. I looked in the mirror and didn't flinch. I found that letting go of the anger I felt about the way I looked opened up a portal to joy that I didn't know was possible. Part of the happiness that people saw on the television on a Saturday night was my own personal triumph that I was doing what I was doing. That I'd defeated my demons and let go of the things I hated about myself.

That's not to say that I don't sometimes lapse. I'm still liable to panic if I have to get dressed up for a TV show or a gig. But my attitude towards my appearance is better than it's ever been. I had to confront all of my fears before I could defeat them. After *Strictly* is over the contestants are allowed to keep one costume if they want to. I asked for my red boots, tiara and glittery superhero dress. I'm getting it framed and hanging it on my wall. It's absolute proof that jumping outside my comfort zone was the best thing I could ever have done.

Be kind to others, but above all be kind to you. You deserve it. You can be Wonder Woman if you want to. I know I am.

CHAPTER 7
TRAVELS WITH MY PLANT: CONTINUED

GREENWICH! Where all clocks are born and raised. Lovely place, lovely people and a show where kindness and joy came together in one venue with one tweet.

> JoMH@missflorapost
> My wife bought me a banjo for my 40th birthday because I've always wanted to play one like Kermit the frog does.

I can't really express just how much I love this tweet. And I adore both of the people in the story. One of them because her lifelong dream was to be like Kermit the frog, and the other because she knew about that dream and bought her a banjo to achieve it. I hope this doesn't seem weird because I don't know either of these women, but I sometimes sit of an evening imagining @missflorapost sitting playing the banjo with a look of complete happiness on her face.

Amy Killen @Amy_Killen
My wonderful friends were a human wall for me when I
had an accidental 2am cry in public.

A more practical act of kindness here. Again, a purely
instinctive act to protect a friend from a public emotional
breakdown. As someone who cries at the drop of a hat I
appreciate this tweet. I'm well known for my propensity
to break down in public, sobbing, wailing and snotting.
And I've always appreciated it when friends have removed
me from a public setting so I can't be seen, and I've returned
the favour for those friends. If you're ever in that situation,
don't panic: there's a very definite way of doing it so it's
not obvious. Gently grab the elbow of the hysterical human
and remove them to somewhere safe. Not the toilet. Never
take a crying person to the toilet. Not only will others
demand entry to the toilet (if it's a single cubicle) but if
it's a large toilet, say in a pub or a shopping centre, it
will simply attract more attention. You'll find strangers
taking far longer than is necessary to go about their business because it's an undisputable fact that any problem
in life is made infinitely more interesting if discussed or
overheard in a toilet.

Elie
A stranger bought me a drink in a pub when I was upset
about a break up.

I find that we've become awfully concerned about
intruding on others' emotions. Maybe it's because of our

inherently 'British' reserve, maybe it's because we're frightened of being lumbered with an emotional person, maybe it's because of the terrifying press coverage of mental illness but it seems like a big thing to simply ask someone if they're OK. But it can really help. Buying them a drink. Patting them on the back. Sometimes the simple fact of knowing that someone cares can really help. This is a lovely story of a simple thing that Elie has remembered.

Francesca Hunt @PrincessFran87
let a drunk lady sleep on my bed @a wedding. Tried2later wake her by lifting the covers. She had stripped. We slept on the sofa.

This is excessively generous – quite above and beyond what most people would do. It's also a salutary lesson in not letting strangers into your house at a wedding. Francesca, I salute you. I'm a kind woman but you are a hero.

Glasgow

My home town and my favourite place in the whole world. The city undoubtedly has its faults, but it is, to me, one of the kindest places in the whole world. I fully expected to receive a lot of kindness stories here and I wasn't disappointed. Many of them couldn't be published as they were possibly incriminating. Here are some that won't lead to legal action:

GiraffeOnAStick @giraffeonastick
My wife @IncognitoLinda has taken all the minging orange Revels for me tonight. That's love.

That is love and that is kindness on a plate. I value kindness above all other traits in a relationship, whether it's with a friend or a partner. And eating something that someone else doesn't like is the ultimate sacrifice. Or making an excuse for someone so they don't get embarrassed. I suffer terribly from stomach ailments and have on occasion felt quite unwell at a party or social occasion. Rather than make me say what's wrong with me so we can leave, my wife, who knows by the expression on my face what's up, will always make an excuse for me. That she needs to feed the cats, or she has an early start, so that I don't need to go through the awkwardness of saying, 'My stomach feels like it's about to fall out of my body.' That's love.

Kai Durkin @firewolfmutt
Tonight, at your show I made it to the bar before I realised I didn't have any cash on me, so a lovely woman paid for my water.

While I'm not suggesting that we all start paying for other people's drinks, there is something lovely about giving a stranger a gift. The unexpected joy of something you were expecting to pay for being given to you. I like to try to make people happy with those sorts of spontaneous presents, but sometimes people are a bit odd about it. On the very stand-up tour I'm writing about now I found myself catching an early-morning train to London from a small-town station. There was a coffee cart open and so I ordered myself a strong beverage. I watched a businessman approach the cart, clearly about to start his morning commute, and I was overcome with a feeling of joy and happiness. I wanted to spread it around (remember it's an HTD) and decided to pay for his coffee so he started his day with a smile. He put in his order and I said to him, 'This one's on me.' He looked at me with suspicion and said, 'Why?' I replied with a shrug and the statement 'Just because.' After another moment of staring he walked away, but only after a brusque 'No thanks.' I think he thought it was some form of sinister trick and I might either a) have drugged the coffee so I could kidnap him and keep him as a sex slave or b) turn round and go 'Ha! It was a joke!' Such events don't put me off though. I will persist in trying to buy people coffee, even if they think I'm a weirdo.

CHAPTER 8
I'M THE IDIOT NOW
AND I LOVE IT

OK, so you've been reading this book and you may be nodding along and having a bit of a chuckle at some of the stories; perhaps you've been wondering how I've managed to function as a human being for as long as I have, but the niggling question that remains is: 'Why on earth should I care – what's the point?'

And I get that. I understand. Why should a book written by a small Scottish woman make any difference to anyone? Why should we even concern ourselves with what's going on in the world? The answer is that I still think we should. We must. For lots of reasons.

The first, and most important one for me, is that – and I can't quite believe I'm actually writing this – it's not all about us. I inhabit the planet right now, but I don't know how long I'll be here. I don't mean I'm about to pop my clogs, but we live here in a temporary way and there are many generations to come who have to spend time in whatever hell-hole we're creating. And if you're young and think, 'Stuff them all, I'll be dead and gone before the ice caps melt and we have to live with our dolphin overlords,' I understand. I used to have no interest in future generations either, partly because, well, I didn't want to breed.

Now I'm not letting my gender down, I'm not making a political statement, I'm not being difficult and all gay about the situation – I just don't want children. I've never had maternal feelings, never had that yearning to be a mother and I've certainly never regretted the fact that I haven't produced a mini-me.

I find not having kids is brilliant fun. For example, I can choose where and when I go on holiday. Friends of mine with tiny humans have to choose their holiday destination based on 'where they can find some food the kids will eat' or 'somewhere we can reach by car because you know they get restless when they fly and last time you didn't help a bit, you just put your headphones on and went to sleep. And who was left with the kids? Muggins. As usual. You said to me when we had them that you wanted to be involved. Well get involved, Brian. Get involved. All I have is my Bikram, Brian. Bikram and gin, Brian. I have a degree in Engineering, Brian!!!'

I do have children if you consider my cats my children. A lot of people don't. But I do. Indeed, I often tell people I have five children. As you'll be aware, the accepted protocol when someone says that they have a child is to ask to see a picture of said child. And I have *many, many* pictures of my cats. In fact, after a recent audit of my mobile telephone device I ascertained that I have 1,348 photos. Twelve are of meals I found particularly visually appealing, 14 are of my wife, 20 are of me trying on hats in shops and 1,302 are of my cats.

The world is, in my view, divided very much into two types of people. Those who, when shown a picture of a cat by someone who introduces said cat as their child, simply nod and smile. And those who, when shown the picture, point out, very clearly, that it's not a child. It's a cat. I don't like those people. They're the type of people who've never sat in the front of a shopping trolley as an adult just to see if they still fit. I have. And I don't. Although it was an excellent way to meet some firemen.

Let me be clear about one thing: I can say, with complete confidence, that I *do not* want, and indeed *never have* wanted, children. Some of you are surely thinking, but why, Susan? You're clearly so maternal. Like the old woman who lived in a shoe. Which I thought was a lovely nursery rhyme about a sweet old lady. Until I re-read it.

> There was an old woman who lived in a shoe.
> She had so many children, she didn't know what
>   to do;
> She gave them some broth without any bread;
> Then whipped them all soundly and put them to
>   bed.

Someone call social services.

I know that it's a very bold statement to say I don't want children, so maybe I should clarify. I mean that I don't want to have children. Not that I don't see how I could have children in a practical sense, not that I'm frightened of having children (although it does look like it might nip a bit), not that, as far as I know, I can't have children, it's quite simply that I don't want to have children. It's a decision – a conscious, well-thought-out decision that I made a long time ago.

Some people automatically assume that my decision not to have children is based on my sexuality. But many gay people have children, despite the protestations of those who believe that same-sex parenting means that we're one step closer to being able to marry our pets. Which, incidentally, would be awesome.

So I don't think you could blame me if my view of how society perceives gay parents isn't all that positive. And it's entirely possible that, subconsciously at least, I've been put off being a parent because of society's attitude. Growing up, I remember the reaction to the book *Jenny Lives With Eric and Martin*. Many of you might remember the scandal caused by this simple children's book about a same-sex couple and their daughter. The stories included Eric and Martin dressing Jenny up like Carmen Miranda, leaving their daughter at home while they went to karaoke and being fabulous all the time. Of course, it didn't!! It detailed the mundane realities of parenthood that occur whether you're gay or straight. A trip to the launderette together, preparing a surprise birthday party and even a woman expressing homophobic disgust when passing the family in the street. As innocuous as it seems now when you look at it, it apparently contributed to the passing of the Thatcher government's Section 28 legislation. I was nine when the book was published in 1983, and like many young people at the time, can't fail to have been influenced by some of the coverage that the book received. The *Sun*, for example, ran the headline 'Vile Book in School: Pupils See Pictures of Gay Lovers'. Tell you what's not vile: the overt objectification of women by printing topless pictures of them in a newspaper. No. That's not vile. That's just outdated and repugnant. But you can play the bingo and that's all good clean fun.

My experience of gay parenting is that it's rarely the children who are perturbed by it. The moral outrage, as always, comes from adults who fear the 'other'. The erosion of society, the creeping menace that homosexuality represents to them. I like the phrase 'the creeping menace of homosexuality'. I read on the Internet that it's the title of the new *Stars Wars* pre-prequel, where Darth Vader goes to football camp in the summer and has an interesting experience around the campfire with his friend Dave. I'm not suggesting that George Lucas is running out of ideas – heaven forbid. Although I have heard that the second pre-prequel is about the tendering process to find a contractor to build the Death Star. It's called *The Procurement Wars*.

It's my firm belief that when talking about gay parents, the 'gay' bit is an unnecessary addition. Well, unless we start describing all parents with an extra adjective. 'Oh look, there's Judy, she's the drunk mum. And Andrew, he's the "cheating swine who's living on his own because he couldn't control his libido" dad.' The only time that it's appropriate to preface anything with 'gay' is when talking about a happy person in the 1930s. Surely it's kinder to simply refer to people as parents. Because let's face it, the definition of what is a family now isn't the two point four children we might have known in the past. Grandparents, aunts, siblings, step-parents, are all family in the eyes of children. Sometimes kindness is about how we change preconceptions.

Some of my friends have suggested that it would be easy for myself and my wife to have children because there are two of us capable of breeding. Like two prize sows at the fair. Maybe we could flip a coin to see which one of us wins: Well done! Instead of a goldfish you've won eighteen years (at least) of financial hell! Why not just burn all your money at the moment of conception? It'll save a lot of time.

People seem to think that two women together would mean that we'd be in broody overdrive, popping out children like the Alien Queen in the film *Aliens*. The expectation that our gender automatically means we'd be chomping at the bit to have kids is as stereotypical as suggesting that all gay people are fabulous dancers. I'm not. I'm an incredibly enthusiastic dancer but if there's one thing we've all learned from Boris Johnson, enthusiasm doesn't make up for a lack of ability.

The truth is that I have never factored in my sexuality when reasoning whether or not I would have children; it's the least important consideration. In fact, no one's opinion about whether or not anything I do is morally questionable has ever stopped me doing anything. A far more important consideration for me is that, despite their size and apparent cuteness, children terrify me.

I'm not frightened of them like I'm frightened of great white sharks or of bears (although if we've learned anything from films like *Child's Play* and *The Omen*, it's that children are terrifying sociopaths at heart). No, I mean that I'm frightened of them because I just don't get them.

For example, I find the honesty of children terrifying. Unlike adults, they haven't learned that the 'truth' is often best left unsaid. Children are blunt and spare no thought for your feelings. I used to do comedy for kids but had to stop when a small child put her hand up during a gig and shouted, 'You're just not funny!' The rest of that gig was quite difficult as I felt like I had the comedy critic from the *Guardian* reviewing me from the third row.

I also don't think I have the personality traits required to be a parent. I've studied people who have kids, and one thing I've noticed is that to have a child you need to have patience. Loads of it. Children interrupt you when you're trying to sleep or eat or have fun. I couldn't stand it. I find it difficult enough to put up with my wife ruining my enjoyment of films. Because one of my greatest loves is rubbish movies – the more awful the better: *Sharknado*, *Mega Shark vs Giant Octopus* . . . I like to watch them in complete silence so as to be absorbed by the experience. Sadly, Chatty McChatface who I'm married to has other ideas.

I was recently watching a film with my wife called *Battleship*, based on the board game Battleship. If you haven't seen the film, then, spoiler alert! In the film *Battleship* based on the board game Battleship, some aliens try to attack a battleship that's stranded in the middle of the ocean. If you've been saving it for Christmas, don't. It's no *Citizen Kane*. It's important to note that the film *Battleship* stars R&B legend Rihanna (of course it does). It becomes very clear, very quickly, that Rihanna is the chef, pilot and rear gunner of the battleship. I accepted this without question and settled down to watch. Within around ten minutes, my wife said, 'That's ridiculous.' I said, 'Why, love of my life? What's ridiculous about it?' She said, 'I'm pretty sure that the US Navy has a more stringent training programme and you'd have to choose one profession to specialise in.' Really – that's the bit you stumbled on? Not the robot alien things. Not the fact it's based on the board game Battleship. Because if that's the thing you're having trouble with, then we're in for a long night.

That wasn't half as bad as the night we watched the film *Bait*. In the film *Bait* a great white shark – yes, a great white shark – gets stuck in a supermarket. Well sure! Why not! For those of you wondering, there's a tsunami, which washes this highly intelligent great white shark into the shop. Now, I wanted to watch it because it sounded amazing for a start and also because I always think it's useful to be prepared for any eventuality. The film progresses as you would imagine. People cowering on top of the shelving units while a super-intelligent shark picks them off one by one. About half an hour in, just as things were really hotting up, my wife said, 'That's ridiculous.' I said, 'Why, love of my life?' And she said, without skipping a beat, 'Because at the start of the film we saw an outside shot of the shop and the dimensions of the front door are such that a shark that size couldn't get through it.' Really? Again?

But maybe more importantly, I've wondered if my antipathy to having children came about because children are also not that keen on me. Whenever I'm in the room with them they sense my unease. Much like cats can sense a human who doesn't like them. My unease around children is made more awkward by the fact that my wife is so very wonderful with them. They swarm towards her like tweets around a scurrilous rumour. She's a natural – reading stories, pretending to be a pirate, playing hide and seek . . . While all this hilarity is happening around my ankles, I sit quietly in the corner. Like a nun on a Club 18–30 holiday.

Not long ago I found myself at a friend's house. She has two children. My wife was in her element with them. When we left my friend said to her children, 'Give Auntie Lee a hug' and they did. They hugged her and hugged her and hugged her. My friend said, 'Give Auntie Susan a hug' and they stood, arms folded, and said, 'No. She doesn't deserve it.' We'll see who deserves a hug when they're sixteen and want their Auntie Susan to buy them and their friends a cheeky bottle of peach schnapps.

Let's be honest, as a woman you are expected to want to reproduce. It starts when we're children. Boys get tanks to play with; girls get dolls and the weight of social expectation. When I say I don't want children the first thing I can see in people's eyes is pity. The automatic assumption is that maybe I can't have children – because everyone wants them, don't they? In my experience, it's really only women who get the pity look. When a man says the same thing, it's simply seen as a valid choice. Perhaps it's got something to do with the fact that gents can have children far later in life than women. Mind you, I'm basing that assumption on my rudimentary knowledge of the reproductive system, which I learned at school. I had my eyes closed throughout the video we were shown, although I do remember shouting, 'Does anyone want a cup of tea?' halfway through.

Women are often put under pressure to have children, too. I once had an awkward conversation with a relative that went like this:

'How old are you now, Susan?'

'Thirty-nine.'

'And no kids?'

'Just the cats.'

'Thirty-nine, eh? Tick tock, tick tock!!'

I believe that's the biological clock that is apparently ticking inside me rather than the onset of a parasitical invasion by death-watch beetles. Of course, there are time pressures on a woman, but there's something very odd about someone commenting on your intimate biological functions. Perhaps women should start saying to men, 'You're forty-five? Nearly time for prostate trouble, eh? It burns, it burns!'

It's true that part of me would like to keep my legacy going. To have an heir to leave my vast riches to. Well, someone to make sure I'm not found dead in my flat eaten by my cat children, at least. But that's just a risk I'll have to take.

As with everything in life, you make your own choices. If you have children, I celebrate that fact; all I ask is that my decision not to have them is also respected. I find great joy sitting in my pants on a Friday night, eating pakora, safe in the knowledge that I don't need to get up at 6 a.m. to take Susan Junior to gymnastics camp.

In my defence, one of the reasons I'm so awful with children is that I've lived most of my forty-three years without anyone in my immediate family having a child. I'm the youngest of three children, and neither my brother nor sister had produced any grandchildren for some time, thus maintaining the status quo of me being the cutest member of the family. And I was perfectly happy maintaining pole position, as the youngest in the family often does. But then everything changed.

I became civil partnered in 2012. It was to be the most important day of my life, and the day when a lady should be the centre of attention, so when I announced the date of my upcoming wedding – 3 June – I settled back for the inevitable tidal wave of family pandering.

And then, without any consultation, without any consideration to my feelings, my sister announced that she was having a baby. And she was due to give birth. On 3 June.

How very convenient! Ignoring the clearly deliberate attempt to ruin my big day, this development caused even greater concerns. This was a child I couldn't easily ignore. It would be genetically linked to me. It would undoubtedly, and inconveniently, appear at family occasions like Christmas. I'd be required, at some point, to hold it. I mean when a friend asks if you want to hold their child it's acceptable to go, 'No thanks, this is a clean jumper' but when it's been yanked out of your sister, there's a certain amount of expectation surrounding your role as auntie. Even before the baby was born, changes started to happen. My parents started to lose their minds at the prospect of having a grandchild. I noticed that my regular phone calls from my mother were becoming less frequent. I started to suspect that the prospect of this baby was more exciting than I was.

I stayed strong. I reassured myself with the knowledge that the child would be cute for a short amount of time and then, slowly, I could reclaim my position as favourite. And I knew that part of the excitement about the new arrival was that we didn't know what brand of child it was going to be – niece or nephew. Apparently it's better if it's a surprise, like a Secret Santa at work. If I was asked what I wanted it to be, which was rare because I was sulking most of the time, I would say that I wanted a girl. At least then I'd have some small chance of having something to say to it when it got to sixteen. Although if it was a boy I was comforted by the fact that I have the full collection of Steven Seagal DVDs. And I could help him with chat-up lines for girls when he got older.

So all we had to do was wait for the big day. Not my wedding, oh no: the birth of the baby Calman. My parents watched out the window for a star to travel across the skies and for three wise men to appear. Of course, just to spite me, my sister was late in delivering and didn't give birth on my wedding day. It was a further two whole weeks before the momentous day finally happened.

I met my niece when she was only a day old, and when I first saw her I wasn't the only one who was trepidatious. We circled around each other; well; I circled around her, she was apparently happy to have our first formal meeting lying down. My sister handed her to me and a rather curious feeling crept over me. I believe it's called 'affection'. Actually, my niece's first contact with her Auntie Susan was to look up and see a blubbering mess. But I suddenly understood it all. I got the stories that you hear about women turning over cars to rescue their children from underneath. Of parents risking their lives to save their kids. This little tiny thing was almost as precious as my cats.

They decided to call her Grace. My middle name is Grace. I was named after my gran, who was also called Grace. I like to think of us as the Three Graces. And I'm not ashamed to say it: she has changed my life. The past six years with her has been amazing. I was a pouncing tiger last weekend. My hip popped out, but I kept going. And I taught her how to burp properly. And when she laughed at one of my jokes it was the best sound in the world. Well, it wasn't my joke. The good thing is she hasn't seen Morecambe and Wise yet. I've done the trick with the paper bag, I've jiggled my glasses, and, when she was frightened by the sirens on an ambulance, I leaned over and gently said to her, 'They won't sell many ice creams going at that speed.'

The point is that I'm the idiot now. I show people photographs of my niece getting on a chair and off a chair, then on it again. I'm the annoying woman who says things like 'She's very advanced for her age, you know.' I sit down with her and earnestly tell her she can be whatever she wants in life. I find myself angry on her behalf. I had to be physically restrained from charging down to her school after she told me the boys in her class had said that 'girls don't play football'.

I roll around the floor for her amusement. I make fart noises, so she giggles. I sing songs, I dance. I've done what I always said I wouldn't: I've lost my dignity. And I really don't care. I still don't want children myself. But I like going round and visiting her, like going to a human petting zoo with one enclosure.

I do *get* children now, and I'd go so far as to say I like them. Kind of. But even though my days of channelling the emotional warmth of the Child Catcher may be over, I still think it's best that I don't have my own. I mean, how embarrassing at morning register to have the teacher call out: 'Andrew, Belinda, Colin, Helen Mirren'. I would totally call my child Helen Mirren. Boy or Girl. But I'm happy being an auntie. And having my niece around has had a strange effect on me, kind of like aversion therapy: I've found myself not hating other children as much. Listening when people talk about how talented their kids are. Thinking that they are really rather wonderful.

I'm happy to visit my niece, and babysit her and, for short periods of time, be responsible for her. But finding one child that actually likes me doesn't remove my concerns. That I would be an awful, short, grumpy parent with a child who'd stand with its arms folded tutting at me because I'd accidentally left it in the frozen-food aisle at the supermarket.

Still, for now I've put aside my dreams of being a competitive-eating champion, because I'm an aunt, and I've got to be the world's most kick-ass aunt possible. Grace is a major part of why I've changed my view of the world, because it's not all about me anymore.

I don't want her to ever live through what I've experienced. To have to suffer discrimination because of her gender, or dismissed by those intimidated by her or to be frightened walking home at night. Nor do I want the world to go down the path it appears to be heading right now. Almost everything I do now is an attempt to make sure that she doesn't have to put up with what I've had to. She shouldn't have to apologise for her opinions. She shouldn't have to put up with sneering comments, or men who use power against her, or think she's fat and ugly because of something some idiot said to her online. The #MeToo movement suddenly becomes even more important when you've someone else to consider. I can take care of myself because I've learned how to, but wouldn't it be absolutely lovely if the next generation didn't have to? If she and her friends didn't sit down on a Friday night when they're older, swapping war stories of bad experiences. I want her to be kind and to experience kindness in return. To not have to battle through life, but to enjoy it.

I don't want her to be limited by preconceptions or glass ceilings. I tell her often that she can be anything she wants. And it's getting through to her. I received this text message from my sister the other day:

Had a great conversation with Grace today – Grace 'Mummy did you know when I grow up I can be whatever I want to be?' Mummy 'yes Grace it's wonderful isn't it!' Grace 'well except a killer – that wouldn't be so good would it?' Mummy 'no – I am really hoping that isn't your career choice!'

When she put it like that, her dream of being a hairdresser-paleontologist didn't seem a bad option. I mean I'm sure she would be an excellent killer, but I'm currently hoping that the hairdresser-paleontologist wins out.

For the first time in my life I am on a genuine crusade to leave this place better than I found it. Because the younger generation needs us. I spoke to some girls in their mid-teens while teaching a course on comedy and their outlook on the world was quite desperate. I asked them what they wanted to do when they left school and instead of answers I was greeted by confused looks. As if asking what their ambitions were was an unthinkable scenario. Did they want to go to college? Get qualifications? Or if they weren't interested in academia did they want to study for a vocational course? Almost all of them looked at me as if I was mad to even suggest such a thing. There was no ambition simply because they didn't see the point of having any. To me they weren't lazy or feckless, they simply didn't see that there was anything they could aspire to. A generation of young people with no hope is a terrifying thing. Their self-respect and confidence were at rock bottom and it was a depressing discussion to witness. What if we listened to people starting out in life and were more empathetic to their concerns? Perhaps then it would be easier to understand their frustration at life and consider what things must be like for them. I find the world very scary at times, but I've at least had a life and a career and own my own home. I can't imagine what it would be like to be facing growing up now.

Even if you don't have a child, or a niece or nephew, it's possible to want more, to want better for where we live. And it can be a local or a global desire. The good thing about kindness and joy that's directed to others is that it forges connections. It can make a difference. And even small changes can result in something incredibly special. Sister Helen Prejean, who I've talked about previously, probably never thought that her individual campaign would inspire a woman at a Scottish university to travel across the world to work with prisoners on death row. But it did. And it inspired many more before and after me. Just because something seems past saving doesn't mean that we shouldn't try.

If I was selfish I would be happy with the way things are. The old 'I'm all right Jack' attitude where you don't care what happens to anyone else as long as you're OK. But I can't do that. The people I admire most in the world are those who have done things to make change happen. The suffragettes who battled for equality. The LGBT advocates who marched against Section 28. Rosa Parks, Malala Yousafzai, Maya Angelou, Ruth Bader Ginsburg, Harriet Tubman. Everyone who has spoken out, marched, shouted and made a difference. I don't go on many marches – not because I don't agree with the causes that they represent, just because I find being in large crowds stressful. But you don't need to march to make a change. Joy and kindness can happen with your next-door neighbour, your work colleague or a stranger.

Unquestionably, not having children made me more selfish. I was looking out for number one. I'm slightly ashamed in a way that it took me so long to wake up to the fact that I needed to be on board to save the planet. The change in my attitude was long overdue and I know, I now sound like one of those terribly preachy people I once hated. So sue me. I want to change the world.

I think we can make things better for everyone. And I think that we should. Even if the problems seem insurmountable we can chip away at them because it's worth the fight. It's worth the struggle to make this place we live kinder and more joyous. I hope you think it's worth the fight too. Because together we could form an army of joy. And what an army we could be.

CHAPTER 9
TRAVELS WITH MY PLANT: CONTINUED

BELFAST is always a delight. It's also personally thrilling for me to play there because I'm usually on drugs. Not because I'm rock and roll, far from it, but because in order to survive the half-hour flight from Glasgow I have to take a lovely cocktail of prescription medication. It means that when I arrive I'm a) slightly high and b) very pleased that I didn't die on the flight. I also like playing there because it's the one part of the United Kingdom where, at the time of writing, there's no equal marriage and shows are always more exciting when there's something at stake, or there's a message that needs to be spread. Gay people aren't allowed to get hitched because of the peculiarity of the devolved administrations and the bigotry of some politicians. Before I started my show, I informed the audience that it would contain references to my wife and if anyone had a problem with that they could leave and they most certainly weren't getting their money back. No one moved, because most people don't care. Politicians should take note. Belfast loved this gay.

Tibbsey @tibbsey00
Drenched. Walking from school. Borrow spare key from
neighbour dripping all over their hall. 1hr later chips
arrive at the door.

This is beautiful because it's a time-delayed act of kindness. And it's doubly excellent because the kind neighbour
has thought of the person long after they've left their
house. They could quite easily have shut the door and
gone back to watching television. Instead they thought,
'Gosh they might be cold and hungry' and took them
chips. Well done Belfast.

Jane Robb @janerobb52
My daughter has perfected a 'kind' look in response to
my 'how does that look?' And a quiet 'No'.

Ah, the deeply personal question that everyone hates.
Asking how I looked in a snazzy jacket was once the cause
of a full-on argument with my wife. I'd asked her to confirm
whether or not my new blazer looked dandy and she said
it looked fine. Fine. Now there's little I hate more in life
than that word. If something is 'fine' it's awful in my view.
It sits between good and bad like a flabby piece of gristle.
If anything I do is described in those terms I know it's
awful. At the Fringe you want to have a show that gets
either a 5-star or a 1-star review. That means that at least
people have some reaction to it. You don't want a 3-star
'meh' show that people walk out of and immediately forget.
This tweeter's daughter has the right idea.

Aberdeen

Aberdeen has some of the most enthusiastic audiences in the country. I stayed behind after the shows to sign books and ended up chatting until they shut the doors of the venue.

Sirene Boutique @SireneBoutique
I once revived a floundering rat with a hot water bottle & dog food.

Of course you did. And I love you for it. Always save the rats. Always.

Laura @MrsLauraSimmons
Our 10-year-old telling his friend not to worry about getting glasses as it's what's inside that counts #kindness

This is a beautiful example of kindness because it comes from the best place possible: it's instinctive and pure. This young person saw a friend who was upset and said something lovely. Such words can have a lifelong impact. Well done on having an amazing kid.

polybore @polybore
A young woman insisted on putting my shopping trolley away for me. Kind but I have mixed feelings about this as I'm only 44.

This is an example of why some people resist making a kind offer. I know that for some young people 44 will seem ancient and we've all heard stories of people offering seats to pregnant woman only to be told that the woman in question isn't pregnant, etc, etc. But this tweeter took the kind gesture in good humour. I often host CBBC shows and realised that all of the contestants on the show were born after the year 2000. Once, I asked them to guess when I was born, and they looked perplexed. When I told them the answer was 1974 there were audible gasps. To them that's a time they almost can't comprehend. I became ancient in their eyes. And I suppose in some ways I am.

Marie Archer @buttongrrrl
Kindness – Crying in an art gallery in the darkness and an elderly gentleman brought me a cup of tea and handed me his hankie.

A cup of tea – a universal kind gesture that solves all problems, at least temporarily. It really does. A nice cup of tea can be the kindest thing to offer someone. And a hankie. How sweet and beautiful.

Orla Shortall @Sparklechops3
We went out and a drunken woman offered us vodka from her plastic bottle, for no other reason than she was drunk and had vodka.

An example of a kind gesture you might not want to accept but made from the purest place possible. I'm drunk – would you like to be drunk too?

Allan Taylor @ataylor_akaMrT
I helped save a strangers dogs life which was choking when I was out on a walk.

You deserve a medal, sir. Anyone who helps an animal is a hero in my book. And to step in and perform a *Casualty*-style rescue is to be applauded. One day they will write a film about you.

Amanda Peters @amanda138a
Struggling to get in my car with a walking frame, some teenagers stopped and helped when many adults had walked past head down.

A positive teenager tweet! Get in!

York

York is beautiful and is also the site of one of the best meals I've ever had in my life. Before I had hypnotherapy and took drugs so I could get on a plane, my wife and I would mostly holiday in the UK. We decided to take a road trip from Glasgow to Monkey World (it's a monkey sanctuary and it's brilliant), Legoland and Portmeirion. They were all my choices so I kindly asked my wife where she wanted to go. 'York!' she cried and so off we went. It was lovely and we had a delicious meal there. I enjoyed all my trips as well. We have a very equal marriage, honest.

Louise LLB @Neostarr
My husband vowing to make me a cup of tea every morning for the rest of my life #kindness

I understand this tweet. Every morning for the past fifteen years I've got up first and made my wife a cup of coffee. I tend to work from home and she has to make her way into town, so I think it only right that before she leaves she enjoys a slurp of fresh brew in bed. I also do it because she won't get out of bed otherwise. I've never encountered someone who sleeps as much as she does. If she could she would sleep till midday and go back to bed at 9 p.m. If she wasn't with me she would get up at 8 a.m. and get the train at 8.10. I'm so used to getting up and making the coffee that it's very much routine. So as a treat, every Valentine's Day I ask for the same thing: that she gets up and makes *me* a coffee. Just for a change. And she nods and the night before, she sets the alarm.

I ask for something simple because I've never been a huge fan of Valentine's Day. Probably because for many years the only person who sent me a card was my cat, although how he reached the postbox I'll never know. I've never found it a problem being a love Grinch because, luckily for me, my wife isn't one for presents or expensive frippery. I usually make her a card with a hilarious photo of me stuck on the front of it, and she always receives it like it's made out of diamonds and gold. I always thought she was just a nice person with low expectations until I discovered why she was happy with such terrible Valentine's cards. It turns out it's all in her genes.

My wife's gran passed away a few years ago, and after the funeral we had to go to her house to clear her belongings and sort her possessions. As we worked our way through the flat we ended up in the bedroom and dug out an old suitcase from the bottom of the wardrobe. It was stuffed full of papers and receipts and all manner of correspondence, none of which seemed on first glance to be of any importance. My wife started to sort through the nonsense and in the middle of it all she found a large plain white box with a ribbon on it. She opened it and immediately started laughing. I stared at her, wondering if the emotion was getting too much, as she carefully lifted out the biggest padded Valentine's card you can imagine. Covered in hearts, teddy bears and flowers, it was, to put it politely, a bit much.

When she'd stopped laughing she explained that it was the Valentine's card that her grandfather sent her grandmother every year. They had been together for decades: he (Jim) was a handsome dark-haired sailor, she (Nan) was a gorgeous woman with an infectious laugh and they loved each other dearly. From my understanding of their relationship, Jim was a typical east of Scotland man who was affectionate but not overly romantic. A man's man, if you will, whose love was expressed in private and not for the world to know about. One year (probably in the early 1970s) in an unusual display of affection, he bought that incredible card for his wife. It was not only an unexpectedly overt gesture but also probably quite expensive for the time. My wife was laughing because she remembered that on 15 February every year Jim would take the card, put it back in its box and safely stash it away. Then on 14 February the next year he would bring it out and proudly display it again. The same card, every year. It's not that he was tight with money, or selfish; he was genuinely so pleased with his purchase that nothing else would ever beat it. And Nan was so overwhelmed by his overt gesture that she adored it too.

The inscription in the card read 'All my love, Jim'. And to be honest, what more did it need to say? One card, one sentence, forever. Nan didn't need money spent on her; she just needed to know how he felt, and he showed it publicly, once a year with a padded card displayed on the mantelpiece for everyone to see.

The anecdote touched me, not only because of the story of Jim and Nan, but because my wife had clearly heard her grandmother boasting of this amazing 'once a year' card proclaiming love. And now, to her, love isn't something that needs refreshing with an expensive card; it means saying something once and meaning it. Reaffirming something that you already know, reminding yourself of the promises that you made.

I know now that I could write 'All my love' on a Post-it note and it would be as good as the most expensive card in the world. Because if you mean it, it's truly all you need to say.

So, every Valentine's Day I wait for my coffee. Every

Valentine's Day she sleeps through the alarm. Every Valentine's Day I bring her a cup of coffee in bed and she apologises. It's our tradition.

Sophie
A friend confiscated my credit card once when I mentioned I was considering buying some Crocs. That was kind.

It was indeed. You should buy that friend a thank you present. Perhaps some Crocs?

Winchester

I seem to recall being very happy in Winchester. The tourist board can borrow that as a slogan if they want: 'Winchester makes you very happy'. You're welcome.

Jill @jillyconnors
I thought I was kind the other day when I told my daughter that wearing pink top and pink trousers made her look like a prawn.

When I was a lawyer I wore a purple suit that made me look like a bruise. I wish someone had told me.

Kate Teacake @kateacake
I am mortally afraid of spiders but pick them up & put them out before my (male) fiancé gets the hoover of death #actofkindness

I sympathise. I am also terribly afraid of spiders. It's because of my gran, as she used to shriek the house down if she saw one and so I developed her fear through osmosis. But I know how important they are to the ecosystem and I don't want to hurt them, so I've developed a coping strategy. I name them. It's a concept I learned from watching *CSI*. There was an episode with a kidnap victim and they suggested that the parents go on television and plead for her release. They urged them to continue to use the girl's name, as if you personalise a victim the kidnapper is less likely to harm them. This is a roundabout way of saying that I find if I name spiders I see them as more human and they become less frightening. If Rodger or Barney are in the middle of the floor I find it easier to gently move them to a place of safety. In other news, I may well watch too much television.

Warwick

Lovely place, Warwick. It's in the middle of a university campus so I walk around with the delicious superiority of a woman who already has a degree.

Sam Chapman @s_chapman89
Shared my sweets with strangers on the train yesterday #kind

I love this. I can't tell you how many times I've had sweet envy when sitting on a train. When someone shares their sweets it's joy personified. I was on the train to

London with my laptop open on the table in front of me. The woman opposite me had some little chocolate rabbits. She saw me looking at them and offered me one. I took it gratefully and gave her a thumbs up. I then put on my headphones and started to work. She stood up at her stop and left the train. A little later, as we approached Euston station, I closed my laptop to see three little rabbits lined up behind the screen that she'd left for me.

Astley Book Farm @AstleyBookFarm
37 yrs ago the stage doorman at Coventry theatre let me into @DollyParton dressing room yes she was there!

I mean, I don't know if Dolly would think this was kind but as long as everyone is OK then that's fine. Just to warn you: if you end up in my dressing room I might be slightly annoyed. I'm usually watching clips of cats jumping on children. I hate to be interrupted.

Rebecca Warner @RFWarner
During bad break up a random woman kept calling me. A wrong number but she always asked how I was. A guardian angel indeed :-)

If this was a romcom these two would have ended up together. But how sweet for someone who didn't mean to call to spend time with someone who's upset. Maybe we could all do with someone accidentally calling us. Unless it's one of those people who call up and ask if we've been in an accident or want a gazebo. I don't think I'd ever want a gazebo. I certainly didn't want one when I lived on the top floor of a block of flats.

> elizabeth goddard @lizgoddard
> Being chased down street by 6' hoodie & unnecessarily low slung jean wearing yoofs, to hand me money I'd left in cashpoint.

Oh my. It's almost as if there's mounting evidence that young people are in fact not that bad. Another tweet about the youth of today being kind. I find that incredibly re-assuring.

> Charlene @NoLoveSincerer
> Radiator was leaking and flooded carpet. Plumber came out on Sunday night still dressed up from date with his wife, fixed radiator and didn't charge us.

For some reason I imagine this plumber dresses like James Bond and it makes me happy. A man in a tuxedo fiddling with a radiator. I had a similar situation recently and the kindness our plumber showed us almost broke our hearts.

We'd been away in Orkney for a few days and our lovely cat sitter had been looking after our cats/kids. We'd recently had some work done in the kitchen and the only bit that was left unfinished was at the top of one of the cabinets. There was no top part to it, leaving the water cylinder exposed and a route to the back of the food larder open. The cats occasionally liked to hide in there and we told ourselves we would get round to boxing it off eventually but what harm could it do?

When we returned from our break we arrived home and, as always, counted noses. We only counted four but that's OK; sometimes the girls like to hide away for a while to punish us for leaving. After an hour I became concerned and started looking for Daisy. After an excruciating search I realised that she had, somehow, fallen head first behind the water tank. She was distressed and upset and I was ready to take a sledgehammer to the wall to get her out. My wife, being calmer than me, instead called the plumber.

It was a bank holiday, it was 6 o'clock at night but he arrived at our house within the hour. He dismantled the tank, drained it and rescued the cat (who was thankfully unscathed by events). As he put everything back together again I asked him how much it would cost and told him it didn't matter the amount as the cats mean everything to us. He shook his head and said he didn't want paying. I pressed him and said that he needed to take some money. His words were 'I don't like making money from sadness.' He asked us to donate some money to charity instead and we did. He's the best plumber in the world.

Michael Butterworth @mike710348
Cancer buggered wife's mobility. At cinema disabled loo broken, queue of 20 backed out so she could go, didn't wait to be asked.

This is toilet etiquette at its best. Even though I am paranoid about toilets (have I mentioned that yet?) I will always step aside if someone more in need appears first. This queue of people quietly and correctly did the right thing. Well done, queue.

CHAPTER 10

You Love Me!

YOU REALLY LOVE ME!
A LETTER OF THANKS TO EVERYONE
WHO VOTED FOR US

THE most amazing thing about kindness and joy is that they can be shared experiences. More importantly, you don't even need to know the person who's happy in order to vicariously enjoy their delight. And even more extraordinary is that the infection can spread without actual human contact. Books, films, music and even television can be the carrier of elation. I like to think of such HTDs as good things, not the bad diseases that you can catch from a door handle or accidentally touching a petri dish full of bacteria. As someone who travels almost constantly, I find myself at the centre of any germ hurricanes that may be on the horizon. I try to stay healthy and packed with vitamins, my rucksack is full of antibacterial hand gel and wipes, but it doesn't stop the inevitable. Sitting opposite someone on a five-hour train journey only to hear the sniffing and the coughing, I know that, at some point, phlegm will come my way. I've found myself staring at a stranger, waiting for the inevitable sneeze like a strange, snotty game of Russian roulette.

One of the most common things people have said to me since *Strictly* is 'You looked so happy when you were dancing,' and I was. I really, really was. I was floating around on a cloud of glee for months, and for someone who has been depressed for her whole life that's quite a change. Perhaps this seismic shift in my mood was the reason why my joy was so completely obvious, and it shone through the fake tan, across the country and into people's homes. But what I didn't expect was that my happiness would make others happy too. I can honestly say that I've never done anything in my life before that's had such an impact on the way that other people felt. Not even the time when I was stuck on a broken-down train for hours and produced a bag of mini Mars bars that I'd, by chance, bought at the newsagents at the station. It's quite amazing to see a grown man tear up at the sight of a tiny chocolate bar. I felt heroic as I walked down the carriage distributing treats with a saint-like nod of the head; my fellow passengers were in a state of joy, but even that couldn't touch the joy generated by *Strictly*.

Oh, before I carry on with this chapter, I know I wasn't the only reason people were happy watching *Strictly*; there were a number of other dancers being utterly brilliant every week. I remember that the first time I saw Alexandra Burke shake her stuff my head almost exploded, and when Ruth and Anton danced the samba I could have died happy right there and then. So, any reminiscences of my time are not made in isolation, but I can only speak of the change in the way that people perceived me. I have no real idea how my fellow dancers (because we were all dancers by the end) felt, although Mollie King did promise to let me live with her in London any time. She may have been being polite.

When I meet people in the street it's often pretty obvious how they know me. As I've said earlier, I do a great deal of varied work on radio and television, often with little crossover between the various genres. Kids know who I am from CBBC, particularly a quiz show called *Top Class*. I'll often see a small child peering at me from behind a chair because they know me as a slightly fearsome but still friendly woman who asks questions. Often people will have read *Cheer Up Love* and want to tell me their own stories of depression. My occasional appearances on *QI* make people think I'm intelligent and that audience will nod at me sagely from behind a copy of Aristotle's latest paperback. I've hosted a few daytime TV shows, so students are often excited to see my face. My appearance on *Countryfile* led to some of the most polite fan mail I've ever received. Radio 4 listeners know me from the topical comedy show *The News Quiz* or my own stand-up shows and they can have a very clear perception of what they think I'll be like. And before I started dancing it's fair to say that I was best known for things like *HIGNFY* or *Mock the Week*, where a group of people sit and make comments on those in the public eye. When it comes to my stand-up or appearances on satirical shows the word most often used to describe me is 'acerbic', although I've never quite understood why that term was used in relation to me. In summary, it indicates biting and sometimes cruel comedy, which is why I dislike it being attributed to me.

I've always felt there's a slightly patronising and sexist undertone to its use because I don't think I'm cruel in my evaluation of the current state of the world, but I do think I have robust views, which for some commentators might be a surprise. It's the old chestnut of men having opinions and women screeching like banshees into the night.

I may not have been likeable to some, but I was moderately successful in what I was doing (whether acerbic or not) and happily trotting along doing it with a certain amount of recognition. People were, mostly, enjoying my comedy and I definitely got the feeling that I was, in some way, raising levels of joy in certain households. The majority of people who came to my stand-up shows seemed to be in better spirits when they left than when they'd arrived. Although I didn't do a proper survey – I think it might dull the laughs if at the end of a show I stood with a clipboard asking strangers to rate me from one to ten. But suffice to say I was doing OK with a large but not immense crowd. Then everything changed. The first and main difference when a show like *Strictly* gets involved is the sheer scale of the audience and the depth of their reaction. It's not just how many people watch it, it's how much they care about it. And the thing is that I get it, I understand that passion. I was a superfan of the show before I went on it; indeed I would plan my entire weekend around it. I've given standing ovations in my living room to past contestants and thrown cushions at the television when Craig gave someone an unnecessarily low mark. But being in it is the most incredible thing, because suddenly you're the person who people invest in, you're the one that viewers vote for and you're the one who makes people feel something.

It meant so much that people cared, and even now, long after the show has ended, I get notes or emails thanking me for cheering people up. I try to reply to as many of them as I can, but there's no way that I can individually reply to every single person who contacts me. Therefore, I wanted to take this opportunity to write a thank you note to all of you. Because it's entirely possible that you will never know quite what you did for me. You may have thought that *Strictly* was a one-way street, but it's not. You changed my life, and this is my love letter to those who watched me dance and made me feel so loved. Because you absolutely did.

You may have already gathered this, but I'm a knowledge nerd. I like to read about everything and anything. In fact, I live my life as if at any moment I might be asked to go on a television quiz show to answer questions in the category 'Everything that's ever happened ever'. When I watch a film, I read all of the credits in case someone, somewhere enquires of me, 'Who was the chief metal worker on *World War Z*?' The answer is Nigel Gray, in case you're wondering. Even when it comes to reading about uncomfortable subjects I'll voraciously devour any information I can get my hands on. For example, my fear of flying has led me to digest many self-help books about the topic, and I scour Internet message boards, use flight trackers and obsessively look at technical diagrams of planes to understand fully how they work.

It's the same with the human brain and soul. I'm almost

evangelical in my crusade to understand how we all work. I've been to spiritualist shows, and therapy, and spoken to countless experts in various fields to understand what and who we are. No area of life has been as written about, theorised and discussed as that of mental health. And the category of self-confidence and self-worth is amongst the most contentious. How do I make myself feel better? How do I love myself? How can I enjoy life without hating myself? Women in yoghurt adverts seem so happy – should I eat more yoghurt? A quick search of online bookstores will show thousands of results for books that promise to help you feel better about who you are. All have tantalising titles like *Pants for Positivity* and *Finding Self-love Through Quilting* or *Stop Moaning and Buck up a Bit, Will You?*

A quick skim of such titles will often reveal similar advice. Things like:

1. You have to love yourself before anyone else can love you.

2. You shouldn't need anyone else's approval to know that you're a good person.

3. Don't rely on others for affirmation; you need to find your own confidence from within.

While I agree with those statements to an extent, I prefer to take a kinder approach to self-confidence, or perhaps a more selfish one. I know that I should shine from within and love myself, not be needy – be a Susan island of joy – but my experience shows that other people loving me does make me feel a whole lot better. It's OK to say that you need others to like you, and it's OK to take joy from that.

Anyone who knows a stand-up won't find my desire for affirmation surprising. The reason that I love comedy and performing is the effect that it has on people. If I didn't need the love of a group of strangers on a Friday or Saturday night, I would be more than content to stay in my house and tell jokes to my cats. To be fair the cats are a tough crowd; they can't talk or laugh and often fall asleep well before the punchline.

In *Cheer Up Love* I was more than happy to state that comedy, in a way, saved me from myself. Not just the audiences but also the art form itself was something that allowed me to express myself in a way I couldn't do before. My first ever introduction to comedy was Billy Connolly. I'd stolen one of his albums (on cassette tape, no less) from my brother, and listened to it on my newly acquired Sony Walkman. I had no idea what stand-up was, no idea what comedy was and no idea who he was. Before long I was doubled over on a train, crying with laughter. People use that phrase a lot, 'crying with laughter', but it's only happened to me on a few occasions, and this, the time I first heard Billy Connolly, was one of them. He was incredible, immense and hilarious. He was talking about places I knew in Glasgow and he was brilliant.

As well as being the first time that I'd heard proper stand-up comedy, it was also the first time I ever remember feeling a new sort of joy. I was elated, in an almost out-of-body way. Breathless from laughing so much and high from the endorphins. That first experience spoiled me somewhat though, because it made me feel that's what all comedy should be. That every audience should leave the theatre feeling like I did. Obviously, they don't – for a start not everyone's Billy Connolly, but also because a huge amount of work goes into making people laugh. Being funny in the pub on a Friday night to people who know you and like you and may have had a few drinks is nothing compared to standing, for two hours, in front of a group of strangers on a wet Wednesday night in February. That takes skill, time, practice and a lot of patience.

I have self-insight; I know when I'm proud of something that I've written, and I know when I'm not. Often people will say to me, 'I saw you at the Edinburgh Fringe when you first started' and I cringe. Because comedy is like anything else – practice makes perfect and I needed a lot of practice. My first few hour-long shows at the festival were the tentative fumblings of an idiot whose only knowledge of what she was doing came from, you've guessed it, a Billy Connolly tape. I'm not ashamed of those shows but I also know that they weren't terribly good at times. On the British stand-up comedy scene, you don't tend to have directors or editors, not unless you're signed to a big agency, and such ignorance often results in a well-intentioned but ultimately flabby show about something that no one is particularly interested in.

My early ventures into the arena of Fringe shows were just that. A mad fumble to find my style and my place in the world of stand-up. Not a complete disaster but nothing to be proud of either. It was only latterly when I realised what I wanted to talk about and started to write shows that reflected my politics and beliefs. My material isn't to everyone's tastes, of course, but I know when I'm proud of what I've done. I can tell from the feel of the room and the sound of the laughter when it's hit the spot and I've done my job well.

If I went along with the school of thought that suggests one should be proud of what one does without requiring the affirmation of anyone else, then no one would ever need to see my shows. I could sit in my house and look at the words and feel amazing. Except that's not what makes me feel amazing. What makes everything better in my life is knowing that people come to the shows and enjoy what I do. I'm absolutely fine with saying that I need other people to love me. I do need a certain base level of self-worth to leave the house, but I'm more than happy to say that the appreciation of a group of strangers makes me jump with joy.

Perhaps that makes me needy and self-centred and maybe even a tad narcissistic but at least I'm honest. To be fair, who doesn't love a compliment? Who wouldn't like someone to come up to them at work and tell them that they're doing a great job? And that's what the audience who watched me dance did. They told me they liked me, and the effect was life-changing.

I'm a very different person to the one I was before *Strictly* because I sort of started to believe that maybe, just maybe, I was someone that people liked. And no, this isn't written for sympathy or for emotional effect; I truly struggle with the idea that anyone has any interest in what I say or do. And I know some people really don't like me or want to listen to me, but that's the joy of the off button. To get to week ten of the biggest show on television was the most surprising and brilliant thing that has ever happened to me. Maybe 'acerbic' Susan wasn't really me.

Unsurprisingly, it was terrifying to begin with. Every week you perform a new dance in front of four judges, a studio audience and over 11 million people. The first stage of terror comes with the judges. Live on television, with adrenaline pumping, you stand, wide-eyed, waiting for the verdict.

Imagine it: standing, waiting to be savaged. Not that it's a new feeling for me since I've been critiqued before – as a comedian I've had hundreds of reviews of my shows published. Some of them had merit, many of them were poorly written pieces of rubbish but that's part and parcel of the job. The difference is that I sort of know how to do stand-up, but I didn't know how to be a dancer. I was being judged on my moves and I really tried my best – my goodness did I try. I practised for eight hours a day, I sweated, I hurt myself, I sobbed, I did everything I could to make my tiny legs do what I wanted them to. I knew going into the show that the judging would happen, that at some point Craig or Darcey would raise their paddles in my face and I'd have to smile through the humiliation. It wasn't that I was disappointed in their comments, it's part of the show when you sign up, but knowing something is inevitable doesn't make it easier. From week one it was clear I wasn't one of the best dancers and every week it didn't get a lot better. While I accepted it and knew my place, I did have glorious dreams of doing something right, of appearing on the dance floor and twirling and sashaying my way to a perfect score. Shirley Ballas would rise to her feet weeping as a new dance talent was discovered. Sadly, that was as likely to happen as the recurring dream I have where I'm announced as the new James Bond.

The judges' marks were only part of the story though, because the audience were the ones who really counted. Through an intricate weighting system, the judges' scores were combined with the audience votes and the two dancers with the lowest scores would compete in a dance-off at the end of the show. When I started, all I wanted was to not go out first and I told family and friends that as long as I made it past week one I would be happy. And much to my surprise, I did. The next target was movie week, because as I mentioned before, that's when you get to go all out with costumes and make-up. We made it there. Next, we wanted to get to Halloween and so on and so on. We kept going. We were bottom of the leader board of the judges' scores almost every week and still we kept going. Because the audience at home voted for us.

I've never gone on any show before where my fate was in the hands of the public because I suppose I never really wanted to know what they thought of me. It's testament to my ingrained fear of not being accepted that I worried that a lesbian in a dress wouldn't be acceptable to the Great British Public. That my quirks and eccentricities would be offputting. I know that some people really didn't like me (thanks Twitter!) but more people did like me. Liked Kevin. Liked what we were doing. In some ways the entirely amateur nature of my attempts was what appealed to people, and I enjoyed that. People could imagine being me, transported from their sofas on a Saturday night to a glittering TV studio to dance for the nation.

The voting figures are genuinely never released to us, so I have no idea what proportion of the public kept us in, but it was certainly significant. Every time someone at home picked up the phone and voted I'm pretty sure that they had no idea what that meant to me, or to any of us on the show. I'd like to thank every single person who voted, because more than any therapy I've ever had it made me more confident as a person.

The people who come up to me in the street and tell me that they like me replace small parts of my soul that slowly disappeared through my battle with depression. All the years of therapy and self-help have never healed me the way that a shake of the hand and a compliment have. The kindness shown to us was remarkable, the joy you gave me is indescribable.

So, if you felt happy watching *Strictly* it was probably nothing compared to the joy that I felt knowing that you were watching. You changed my life and I need you to know that.

Thank you.

CHAPTER 11
DON'T HATE BEING HAPPY

IT'LL ONLY MAKE YOU MORE MISERABLE

OK, so I've sort of persuaded you that kindness and joy are brilliant things and we need more of them. But what do we do about THEM? You know, THEM. The ones who don't want us to be happy. The ones who live in the darkness looking for any reason to destroy positivity. The lemons of the world who look for any excuse to squeeze a bit of bitterness into the sweet sauce of life. You know the kind of people I mean. THEM!

You'll be aware from reading this book that I am always honest with you, my dear readers, and I'm happy to reveal my personal faults and issues at the drop of a hat. So, in the interests of full disclosure I need to tell you I've been that lemon at times. I've sneered at friends who tell me in great detail of the joy they get from their hobbies or interests because I don't understand the point of them. I've been a scoffing, dismissive person in my time, rolling my eyes at the concept of crochet or the joy of jam-making, so I get how easy it is to sink into a quagmire of cynicism. In many ways it's easier to be negative than it is to be positive but as I get older and have lived more, I realise what a mistake I've made. That being negative is a waste of energy. In fact, my change in attitude is so dramatic that when I see negativity now it makes me angry, which is a terrible irony. Let people be happy, I cry! Leave them alone to enjoy their collection of Care Bears/life-size cardboard cut-outs of the Queen/potato sculptures! My crusade for kindness and joy is so important to me that not only do I want to make people happy, I want to stop those people who prevent happiness. I want to (peacefully) destroy lemons. Figuratively, I mean. Real lemons can be delicious and are vital in seafood dishes.

It's not a modern phenomenon to want people to be miserable – I'm sure that back in caveman days someone made a painting of a particularly lovely dinosaur, only to have a passer-by remark on how fat the dinosaur looked – but these days it is easier. For example, comedy, which is in essence something that should make people laugh and by extension make people happier, can actually make people really, really angry. Not just on social media either – in pubs and workplaces all over the country discussions take place that often end in the question: 'But why do you like that show? It's awful. It's just not funny'. Speaking of which, I've always been slightly confused by the desire people have to tell me I'm not funny. I remember standing outside my flat in Glasgow one day, waiting for a taxi. A bin lorry was on the other side of the road and the driver was in the cab. He stared at me with that stare people have when they recognise me and want to say something. I can sense the negativity from these looks because if someone likes me they tend to just come up and say it. Those who stare are different. They have a point to make and they are going to make it whether I like it or not. I panicked slightly but couldn't run away or I'd miss my pick-up, so instead I turned my back and looked at my phone. Usually such tactics prevent the casual remarker from approaching but not this man; he was determined. I heard the door of the lorry closing and turned round to see him casually stroll across the road. The conversation went something like this:

Him: 'It's you, isn't it?'

Me: 'Maybe?'

Him: 'It is. That comedienne.'

[*Side note: when people call me a comedienne I can hear the sarcasm in their voice. I hate it. In the same way I hate being called a 'female' comic. You may as well substitute the word 'female' with the word 'shit'. Sorry, I digress.]

Me: 'I am a comedian, yes.'

Him: 'No offence, love, but I don't think you're funny. Tell you who is funny . . .'

What followed was a list of very good comics and I stood, politely, and listened to why they were great, and I was awful. I like to be polite to people even when they are being rude to me. What else was I to do? Shout about how complex comedy is? Flick his ear and remind him that some of the greatest artists in the world were unappreciated in their time? Tell him I wasn't interested in his views and just wanted to get in a cab and go to the dentist? I did nothing but listen as he finished his list of comics he liked, wished me luck and went back to the bin lorry. I got in my taxi and as it drove away I sighed. When life gives me lemons I'd prefer a gin.

Don't get me wrong – it's fine to have an opinion on *Mrs Brown's Boys* or Peter Kay or whatever comedy happens to be on the television or radio; opinions are brilliant and worthwhile, but the step beyond that, the one I hate, is the desire to make people feel stupid or wrong for liking something different from what you like. No one has the right to rain on someone else's parade. You find the subtle satirical humour in Voltaire's *Candide* delightful? Good for you. But I really like looking at YouTube videos of cats jumping on children. And I'm not stupid because of it. The idea of deliberately stopping joy in its tracks seems to be almost a sport these days. It's a badge of honour to deliberately bring someone down, and people do it for many different reasons.

The first and to my mind most annoying kind of joy-haters are the snobs: those who suggest that the thing that brings the joy isn't worthy enough. The ones who believe that some things (and people) are stupid and irrelevant and not sufficiently intellectual. They are the most frustrating lemons you will ever meet.

As before, I'm going to admit to the fact that I have, in the past, been guilty of intellectual snobbery. But my epiphany about the stupidity of my ways happened way before my time dancing. I went from pseudo intellectual to proud defender of popular culture. You see I used to pretend to have read Chaucer so that people would think I was clever, because then I would be someone to admire and adore. Now I firmly believe that if you're into *Buffy* you can be just as smart as someone who's all over Brecht. Intellectual snobbery is the one thing that makes me angry enough to Hulk Smash in public.

The first time I became aware that some things were considered better than others was when I was very young. In the days before satellite, cable or even Channel 4, the only viewing choice was either the BBC or ITV. And the main channel battleground was the Saturday morning children's shows. In the early 1980s you could watch either *Swap Shop*, a gentle and polite show where received pronunciation was celebrated by Noel Edmonds and his cheerful jumpers, or the epitome of evil, *Tiswas*. If you weren't around at the time, *Tiswas* was a cross between the riots of 2011 and a medieval tournament. It was notorious for its wild nature that encouraged, some parents said, bad behaviour amongst their own children. And so, like many children of that time, the Calman children weren't permitted to watch it. My mum said that the BBC was more appropriate viewing; the subtext was that the BBC was the 'right' kind of channel for us to be watching – proper television that was educational and didn't represent a threat to our very souls. It was clear, in the view of some, that ITV was the equivalent of a brain leech, sucking all semblance of decorum and class out of young people. I think my mum was terrified I would descend into criminal behaviour and throw a custard pie at her like the Phantom Flan Flinger (her concerns very much overestimating my ability in the kitchen). And I'd never do something like that. Why waste a perfectly good custard pie assaulting someone? To summarise, paraphrase and exaggerate my mum's position, watching ITV would lead to prostitution. No doubt.

While I didn't fully understand why we weren't allowed to watch *Tiswas*, I did understand that there was a perceived difference between the two shows based on their content and tone, and that those who watched *Tiswas* were considered wilder than those who enjoyed *Swap Shop*. In my later years I've realised that my friends are divided along the *Tiswas/Swap Shop* line. Turns out that those who watched *Tiswas* considered those who didn't to be wimps. They're right.

Throughout my childhood I encountered similar incidents. For example, my brother, who proudly displayed his collection of Sex Pistols singles, sneered at my purchase of Roland Rat's 'Rat Rapping'. What I understood quite clearly, even though I didn't know what it was called, was that some aspects of culture were considered better than others and that you would be judged based on what you liked.

For many years I bought into that exact concept. While I was at university I suggested to a woman I quite liked that we go to a Fellini marathon at my local arthouse cinema. She was studying film and television at university and lived in London, which was the most exotic of combinations, so I thought I'd pick something that was considered, academically, to be 'worthy'. I thought 'liking'

Fellini films gave me a certain amount of gravitas and therefore, as a matter of logic, she would see me as someone with taste, class and style, and fall in love with me. I really wanted to go and see the Indiana Jones marathon that was on at the same time but I'm an idiot and instead of buying tickets to see an enjoyable romp we saw many hours of what I thought was self-indulgent nonsense. I know exactly the point at which the date went wrong. It was the moment when I clearly and loudly exclaimed, 'This is pish,' much to the consternation of the rest of the audience. I sneaked in to see Indiana Jones by myself. It was much better.

The problem was that I'd picked up from a very early age, from the adults around me like teachers and parents, that if I was trying to impress someone, pretending to be more intellectual was the best course of action. And for a while I saw merit in that belief, partly because the truth of my life is often far from classy. Ask me what I got up to last weekend and intellectual Susan would say, 'What did I do at the weekend? Quite quiet really. Friday night there was a chamber music recital at the arts centre, Saturday afternoon I made some artisan cheese and Sunday I repaired an eighteenth-century tapestry.' The reality would be: 'The weekend? Quite quiet. Friday I went home, and then I sat on the sofa in my pants playing *Grand Theft Auto* until Monday. I drank beer.'

We all acquire our own personal views of what is considered 'worthy' from a variety of sources. Parents, friends, academic influences. But wherever your own line in the cultural sand is, the issue is the same. Intellectual snobbery.

It may sound like a leap, but a boycott of commercial television to protect your child from a life of crime is an example of the concept. It's about the cultural things in life that are considered to have worth, and those that are easily dismissed. Snobbery is quite an easy concept to understand, and it can be seen in something as simple as the way people judge the plastic bag you hold. My league table goes Waitrose/M&S/Sainsbury's/Tesco/Morrisons/Aldi/Lidl/Iceland/blue plastic bag you get in a corner shop. If you're sitting there saying you haven't judged a person based on their plastic bag, you're lying. Also, if you haven't put a cheap present in an expensive plastic bag from a posh shop, you're a fool. It works every time.

Intellectual pursuits are often considered to be things like classical music, opera, theatre and poetry. Things that one can discuss in a voice that sounds slowed down, usually in sentences that make little sense and a laugh at the end of them: 'Of course, when it comes to Beethoven one must never forget his love of wa ha ha ha.'

The first time that I remember encountering the actual term 'intellectual' was when I read *The Secret Diary of Adrian Mole Aged 13 ¾* by Sue Townsend, still one of the best books about teenage angst ever written. Adrian was desperate to be admired and saw the life of an intellectual as a way to attain that admiration. He wrote, '*Now I know I am an intellectual. I saw Malcolm Muggeridge on the television last night, and I understood nearly every word. It all adds up. A bad home, poor diet, not liking punk. I think I will join the library and see what happens.*' Needless to say, I didn't really get the joke at the time. I didn't know what an intellectual was or even who Malcolm Muggeridge was. If you're reading this with a similarly blank look on your face, then let me enlighten you: Mr Muggeridge was a commentator and author known for his witty sound bites. One that I particularly enjoy is his view on current affairs: 'All new news is old news happening to new people.' I looked him up on the Internet, because that's how you find out about everything, and my favourite part of his Wikipedia entry is where it says, 'He is credited with popularising Mother Teresa'. If I was Mother Teresa, I think I'd rather hope that my actions alone would have been sufficient for me to become popular. But humanity can be so fickle, can't it?

Often the terms 'high' and 'low' culture are bandied about when discussing what is 'intellectual' and these are, to me, part of the reason why such snobbery is divisive and destructive. In academic discourse, when referring to the status of cultural items, usually in the arts, if something is considered high culture then it's held in high esteem. Thus, if something is low culture it is something inferior. Often, this term is applied to the culture enjoyed by the less well-educated, the masses – philistines, to use a particular favourite word of mine. But whether something is low or high culture is a decision often made by Professor McProfessor Face from Sponge Pudding College Oxford.

Having already admitted that I bought into the whole snobbery thing myself, when, then, did I learn to stop worrying and love *Strictly Come Dancing*? Quite simply, it was the day I realised that life's too short to read Tolstoy.

Let me set the scene. One rainy Monday afternoon at the height of summer in Glasgow, I was huddled by the radiator in my study, determined, once and for all, to finish *Anna Karenina*. Or at the very least get past the second chapter. Why? Because I'd seen it on one of those awful '100 books you have to read' lists you find in newspapers that are primarily designed to make you feel stupid first thing in the morning. People post them all the time on Facebook. Last time I did it I just ticked them all: 'Susan has read 100% of these books'. But after posting my 'result' I started to wake up in a cold sweat in case one day someone questioned me about the detail of what I said I'd read. 'What did I think of *War and Peace*? Well, it was quite warish and then, em, quite peaceful.' So, I started to read *Anna Karenina* – not for pleasure, but as one of these silly books I had to wade through, like a torturous second job.

As I was reading the first page I heard laughter from the street below. The neighbour's children were playing a game of three and in, which if you don't know requires a football and two jumpers to serve as goals. I loved three and in; I didn't love *Anna Karenina*. I was spending a valuable hour of my life, forcing myself to read something that was considered worthy and educational, and outside people were having fun. As I put on another jumper I realised that it was like being offered two choices of dessert. A healthy fruit salad, or a bowl of whipped cream topped with pouring cream with a cream jus. When one is trying to impress others, one will have the healthy option, but all we really want to do is shove our faces in that bowl of cream until we absorb it through our eyeballs.

I sat at my desk and realised that I'd wasted a ridiculous amount of my life trying to be more intellectual to impress people. Almost as much time as I'd wasted trying to learn double Dutch skipping. (I know. I'm full of surprises.)

People often say life's too short but, in my case, it really is! Not because of my height, you heightists, because of my lifestyle. I'm a high-risk individual. I travel a lot, I have high stress levels and I may partake of bad things. The last thing I want is to spend my final moments whispering to my loved ones, 'But tell me . . . what was the mystery of Edwin Drood?' I want to die at Graceland in the jungle room wearing one of Elvis's jumpsuits.

High culture doesn't seem to have the fun factor. 'I went to Wagner's Ring Cycle on Tuesday. It took the whole day. I got a blood clot from sitting down for such a long time, but it was worth it. What's it about? Haven't got a bloody clue.' Compare the audience at a performance of *The Cherry Orchard* with the punters at a *Doctor Who* convention. It's night and day. Perhaps they should swap round one day. I'd love to sit at the National Theatre next to a Dalek watching some Chekhov.

Low culture is, as I said, often deemed inferior to high culture. Something for the masses to enjoy, rather than the few. And a possible continuation of that logic is that if something is popular amongst the many, it cannot possibly be as good as something that's enjoyed by a smaller, more educated elite.

Intellectual snobbery isn't just limited to the realms of

the arts either. Snobbery can rear its head in reviews, articles or the comments section of the newspapers. In fact, there are seemingly few aspects of our lives that aren't open to judgement and even the simplest acts can involve snobbishness.

For example, the act of ordering a drink. When I go out, people often comment on the fact that I like a pint of beer and I have, in the past, been called common because of it. The simple fact is that I don't like any other alcoholic drink. I hate spirits, especially the ones that move my furniture about, and I detest the taste of wine. Should I really pretend to like a drink that I don't to fit in and be seen as classy, or should I drink what I want in the knowledge that most people actually couldn't tell the difference between a two-pound bottle of wine and one that costs the same as a family hatchback? To me a classy drink is Babycham, but the fact I don't drink it doesn't mean that I'm going to make a show of myself at a fancy party.

The pressure to be seen as intellectual, so you don't seem unintelligent, is ever present, and sometimes people pretend to like things because they feel they should. I don't mean things you *have* to lie about, like saying that the homemade birthday card your child gave you is nice, or a soup that your partner makes for you, which makes you want to be sick, is delicious. I mean plays, books, poems, films and the like. People are so concerned about wanting to like the right things that they ignore the fact that they don't actually like them. It's difficult to be honest, I know, so I'll start. I really, really don't like *Wuthering Heights*. I find the bodice-ripping, repressed emotion dull as dishwater. Kate Bush song, yes! Book, no. Same with Thomas Hardy. And opera. And most classical music. I've tried, believe me. I've put on a smoking jacket and puffed on a pipe while listening to Radio 3 as much as the next woman, but all I can think is *I wish this was Girls Aloud!!!*

But why do I get so upset at the judgements people make? Simply because when one person looks down on another's taste in music or films, they're looking down on the whole person. Just because I like 'low culture' doesn't mean I don't have a brain. I now take personal offence at the association of popular culture with stupidity. As the classic *Dirty Dancing* line said, 'Nobody puts Susan in the corner in a dunce's cap.'

Of course sometimes you just have to stay in your lane when it comes to knowledge. I was on *Celebrity University Challenge* recently. It became clear very quickly that there were holes in my knowledge of what was considered appropriate *University Challenge* material. If it hadn't been for one of the members of my team – Sir Harry Burns, the Chief Medical Officer for Scotland – we would have struggled. I got one question right, which was, unsurprisingly, about films. And not *Citizen Kane* or some other film that you might find on the list of '100 greatest films you have to see'. No, I answered a question about the film *Super Size Me* where Morgan Spurlock eats fast food until he almost dies. By some quirk of fate, we got through to the semi-finals of the competition and by the time we got to that stage I was so perturbed by the thought that I would look like an idiot that I started pressing the buzzer just so I could say something. Jeremy Paxman, who hosts the show, is a very pleasant fellow but utterly terrifying when you're facing him. Time was running out for us, and I was determined to answer a question, to win the points needed for the University of Glasgow to sail through to the finals of the show. Jeremy started the question; I decided I would buzz no matter what.

'What is the correct chemical name for—?'

BUZZ!

'Calman, Glasgow.'

Silence. I shouted the first thing that came into my head: 'Cabbage!' Jeremy fixed me with his famous stare. 'Calman. Do you actually have a degree?' To be honest I wasn't sure myself at that point.

What could be more intellectually intimidating than *Celebrity University Challenge*? Why, *Celebrity Mastermind*, of course! I was asked to do it a little while ago, and sadly I couldn't because I wasn't free on the filming dates. I was actually quite glad. The key to *Mastermind* is the specialist subject, and there's no point in lying about it: we've all judged the person on the television based on what their specialist subject is. It put the fear of god into me because I couldn't answer one question about something like neoclassical Roman architecture, never mind a minute's worth. Before I turned it down, I had a sleepless night wondering about what I could admit to the viewing public that I, Susan Calman, was an expert on. The list I made of possible specialist subjects were:

1. *Cagney & Lacey.*

2. Lesbian tennis players.

3. Thimbles. Because I used to collect thimbles as a child.

4. *Casualty:* 2012–13.

5. Best public toilets I've used.

6. James Bond films where I would've made a better James Bond than the actor playing James Bond.

7. 70s food (Angel Delight and vol au vents).

I think I saved us all from an awkward evening.

Knowledge is everything. To learn about life and history and society is a privilege that many fight and die for. To hear the story of Malala Yousafzai, the Pakistani school-girl who was shot in the head simply because she wanted an education, is a shock to the system that should make us all consider our own positions.

Sir Francis Bacon allegedly said, 'Knowledge is power' and he's right. If we get people to engage in political thought, does it matter whether they do it through reading the *Times* or through watching *Mock the Week*? If we want a population to enjoy science, surely the feel-good enthusiasm of Professor Brian Cox is as worthy as boring them to death with a textbook.

The world needs intellectuals who win Nobel Prizes. But the world also needs the pub philosophers and popular culture that shapes society when it refuses to move by itself. University is an important step in life, but it doesn't mean you can run the country, or even a city, or even your own life. Just because you know big words doesn't mean you're more intellectual than someone who simply gets to the point. In fact, if you use twenty words when ten will suffice you're actually just quite annoying.

We should never stop aspiring to learn, but perhaps we should all dip our toes in a different kind of knowledge pool. Maybe then we could all find some common ground, instead of the chasms being created by wealth and class.

And when I'm on *Mastermind* next year with the specialist subject *Anna Karenina*, don't judge me. I'm just trying to impress you.

People often try to kill others' joy because they don't think that the joy-providing activity is worthy enough. My proposition is simple. If it brings you joy it is always worthy enough. Some of my friends are obsessed with posting videos on Facebook of people falling over. That makes me very nervous as I sometimes fall over, and I'd hate to be one of those people who are filmed and forever after laughed at by people in pubs. But I don't dislike the idea because it's not important enough. A friend of mine loves Judge Dredd. For his birthday I gave him a handmade helmet of his hero and when I gave it to him I thought he was going to cry with happiness. He wears it when he's doing the washing-up and I adore him for it. He's a man in his mid-forties with a very responsible job and all he wants is to dress up while doing the chores. I love walking round art galleries, but I also love *Doctor Who* almost more than anything else in the world and I will fight (metaphorically, clearly) anyone who suggests that the show isn't decent because 'it's just a stupid kids' sci-fi show'.

When so many lemons are about it makes people ashamed of what they like. Such negativity has to have an impact on the happiness experienced. I was at the gym the other day and after a particularly sweaty class a man came up to me. He whispered in my ear, 'You did awful well in that dancing show.' I thanked him, and he walked away. Then he stopped and turned to me with a panicked look in his eyes. He came back over to me and said, 'Don't ever tell anyone I watch it,' and scuttled away like a frightened rabbit.

Don't be ashamed of what makes you happy. Don't let others ruin your joy by making what you like seem unworthy of appeal. And if you are a lemon, stop ruining people's fun. You do what you like, and we will do what we like. I'm no less of a person because I binge-watch old episodes of *3-2-1*. It's one of the most difficult shows on television. I'd love to see Jeremy Paxman try to solve those riddles. Then we'd see who had a degree.

As well as those who sneer at joy because it's come from an 'inferior' source, there's also the negative lot – the 'Unless everyone is happy, then no one should be' type. You'll have encountered these folks; they're the ones who cloak the world in negativity, deliberately trying to pop the balloon of joy. Strangely enough these kinds of people make me smile, because they really are the biggest lemons of all.

For example, if one tweets:

'So excited! Going on holiday!'

One might receive the reply:

'Good for you. So many in the UK can't afford holidays or even food.'

Absolutely fair comment, but it does leave one slightly shy about expressing joy. From experience I know that these people are some of the most difficult to argue with because they are quite correct. Some people can't afford things that make them happy. Some people are living in poverty and misery. But for all of us to stop being happy because of that is a miserable way to live. There has to be a balance where we retain a social conscience while still being able to be happy in our own lives. Almost anything can be turned to misery if you try. My theory, espoused at the start of this book, is that the world is a miserable place at times and that we have to grab joy where we can. We also have to allow people to have that joy.

If your first instinct when someone tells you something happy is to tell them why the happy thing isn't actually that happy – stop. Just stop. Let them be happy. Believe me, if you try to eliminate negativity from your own life it'll make you happy too. Remember the words of the classic television show *Why Don't You? Why Don't You Just Switch off Your Television Set and Go Out and Do Something Less Boring Instead?*

To paraphrase: Why don't you stop bringing everyone

else down and go out and do something less boring instead?
Leave the rest of us to jump up and down.

Now, for the majority of my life I've been depressed
and unhappy. But I would hate it if everyone had to be
miserable because I was; if I see someone who is happy
I want to let them stay that way. Such positivity is easier
to talk about than to live, though. And some people are
happiness-killers because they are just plain old-fashioned
jealous. Jealousy comes from a very bad place, the darkest
place of all in many ways, but this horrible emotion is
one that I completely understand. One of the most difficult things for a comedian is that gnawing feeling when
watching a contemporary doing well. Comedy is a particularly envious trade, full of bitter old hacks willing to
dismiss the success of others with a cursory swipe of the
hand. I always thought if these people spent as much time
writing jokes as they did bitching perhaps they'd be doing
better in their career. But I too have succumbed to such
feelings in the past and they are awful; they leave a person
unable to share joy with a fellow human, incapable of
simply enjoying another person's happiness. More than
that, jealousy can lead to a desire to destroy positivity,
and that's so easy to do. A word, a comment or a sneer
is all it takes. And don't we all know it.

There is a terrifically British part of our psyche that
doesn't really like to celebrate people doing well or being
happy. We love an underdog but as soon as that dog gets
a bone and wags its tail it becomes annoying. Not that I
have to deal with people being intimidated by my 'fame'
in Glasgow. Personally, I love the lack of fawning where

I live. When it was announced that I'd be taking part in *Strictly*, a man shouted across the supermarket at me:

'Good luck wee yin. We'll be rooting for you even if you're shite.'

Which is the most delightful good luck message I've received. They were there for me but they weren't expecting a lot. In my mind that light-hearted cynicism was different to the deliberate negativity that I've seen so much of in my life and on social media. Initially, it confused me. Until I realised one absolute truth: some people are just not very nice. They enjoy being horrible to others and that brings them joy. This book is about finding and celebrating joy in (nearly) all its forms, but I draw the line at this one. Joy in making others miserable isn't right. Schadenfreude to an extent is understandable. A frisson of satisfaction when someone gets their comeuppance is generally OK, but actual pleasure in making people miserable is not.

Therefore I'm going to directly contradict what I wrote a couple of pages ago (I did warn you at the start of the book that I might do this) by telling you that joy isn't always good. If it comes from a place of negativity it's not the kind of happiness I want to embrace. My search for kindness started with surrounding myself with positivity, and with people who feel the same way. On social media I mostly follow people who I know won't be rude or inexplicably nasty to strangers. I watch friends' Twitter feeds and pre-emptively block those who cause them trouble. I try my best to enjoy the success of friends and even strangers with a happy heart.

True kindness is allowing others to have joy in their lives. It's not easy, but relieving yourself of negativity is a blessing on all fronts. Living life with positivity can be difficult and can take some time to get used to, but it's worth it. It might be one of the only occasions in your life where you want to catch something. Those HTDs spread quicker to people with an open mind and a light heart.

I don't like to make threats, but I will leave you with one non-negotiable fact. I always judge people on one criterion: would I want to go on a caravan holiday with them? If you're the type of person who randomly tweets women that they're fat, or who sends abuse to people just because they're on the television, you're not welcome in my Lunar twin axle. Let people be happy. Let them have joy. If you don't, you won't be spending a damp week in autumn in a caravan park in Greenock with me. I know. Think on that, buster.

CHAPTER 12
TRAVELS WITH MY PLANT: CONTINUED

BUXTON

@AndreaGoodinson
This AM we saved 3 baby rabbits from being run over
by our car. I got out & guided my partner slowly past
#actsofkindness

Often acts of kindness occur when people simply slow
down. Instead of driving or walking past something, they
stop. And do something. This audience member could
easily have driven on, but they didn't, and I love them for
it. A couple of years ago I was at the Edinburgh Fringe,
not performing but still working. I was watching shows,
meeting producers, just generally being really important.
I had a particularly important meeting to go to one day
and was hurrying to my appointment when I looked down
and saw a stationary bee. I knew that wasn't how the bee
should be, and I knew that I had to take action. But I had
a meeting to go to. The choice was simple: save the bee

and hope that the person I was meeting would understand because bees are amazing OR go to the meeting and think constantly about the bee and hate myself for not trying to save it. There was no choice. The casualty was on the pavement outside a posh hotel, I ran in and demanded a saucer of sugar water from reception. The staff looked at me strangely, which enabled me to shout loudly, 'There's no time to explain, we have to save the bee!' Through fear or concern for wildlife (who knows which) a saucer of sugar water appeared, and I shepherded the tiny creature to a safe space and the refreshing drink. I saved the bee. And the person I was meeting totally understood. And if they hadn't I wouldn't have wanted to work for them anyway. Always save the bee.

Bristol

Bristol is one of my favourite places to gig. There's something delightful about the place and I ended up doing two shows in a lovely venue with wonderful people. It's also, as it turned out, home to some very kind folk indeed.

Cat Conley @catrin91
Someone found my wallet and went to the effort of tracking me down online to return it.

You often see these stories online with the tag line 'This has restored my faith in humanity'. But it does. The expectation now is that if you lose your wallet or your phone, someone has stolen it, your bank account will be raided and you're in trouble. Instead of the unexpected outcome, which is that it'll be found and returned, we automatically assume the worst. This kind of thing makes a difference.

Bethan @bethkate90
Not a grand gesture of #kindness really but every patient who asks me how I am before I can ask them how they are.

It is a grand gesture because it's about communication. About opening our eyes and actually seeing the person before us. About checking how people are and listening. It's wonderful.

edward hofman @edwardhofman
Kindest thing: someone checked me for a testicular lump; we didn't even know each other very well then. Best friends now.

Friendships start in unlikely places.

Joceline Bury @JocelineBury
The sweet Japanese student who told me that my coat AND skirt were tucked in my pants. No one else had bothered.

STOP LETTING PEOPLE WALK AROUND WITH THEIR PANTS SHOWING! WHAT IS WRONG WITH YOU PEOPLE?

Laura
I fainted on my way to uni and a kind Bristolian stopped
and gave me the Pepsi he'd just bought #kindness

This story isn't just about giving someone a sip of Pepsi;
it's about taking the time to care for someone else. If you
notice, Laura doesn't know the name of the person who
helped her. He was like Batman swooping in and helping
her out. We could all be Batman if we wanted. You don't
even need a costume. I mean I have a costume, but that's
just because I look amazing in it.

Kate Scott @KateseeScott
Went home ill from work. Threw up on platform at Belsize
Park. Tube staff cleaned it up, offered to walk me home
#kindestact

The embarrassment that we suffer when we need help
is often the worst part of any event. I know when I've
been ill it's the fear of people judging me that can stop
me from wanting to bother anyone. The act of quietly
cleaning up vomit and then checking if Kate needed assis-
tance probably helped more than they knew. The psycho-
logical lift you get when someone is simply nice is
invaluable.

Jane McGrath @JaneLMcGrath
Kindest thing: a man in a cafe made a balloon penguin
when I was sitting in a corner trying to cry discretely.

This is just one of the sweetest things in the world. I know I'm often a bit worried about what to do when I see someone who's upset, mainly because I know I'm sometimes difficult to comfort when I'm in a similar situation. When I break down in tears I can see my wife circling me, trying to judge whether to comfort me, leave me alone or try to cheer me up. It's even trickier when the person in question is a stranger. Which is why this unknown man is an absolute hero. I'm surmising his thought process, of course, but I like to think that he saw Jane and, not knowing quite what to do, decided, on impulse, to make the balloon penguin. I think that would help me in almost any situation.

kate
Because the toilet queue was massive (& my pelvic floor is fucked) a lady showed me a secret toilet xx

Access to a secret toilet. Surely one of the greatest acts of kindness possible. As I'll explain later in this book, one of my greatest fears in life is not being near a toilet and large queues for facilities fill me with dread. Imagine the joy if someone just tapped you on the shoulder and said, 'Pssst. We have a secret toilet just down here.' God bless people who know the location of secret toilets.

Birmingham

Birmingham is always a joy to visit. I once performed in a working men's club and a woman in the audience offered to give me a lift home. I wouldn't normally have said yes but she had a convertible and I'd never been in one. She drove me to my hotel and let me have the top down despite it being February. I felt like I was in *Hart to Hart*.

> Rachel holly edwards @rachelholly35
> The kindest thing my partner did is agree to marry me.
> I suffer from anxiety and depression and I am not the easiest person to love.

This is a really interesting view of kindness. Having depression myself I know I often think people are kind because they spend time with me. It's a result of such a hideous lack of self-confidence that I don't understand why anyone would want to be with me for more than five minutes. I remember this tweet well because I read it out on stage and then spoke to the woman who sent it. I believe I said something to the effect that she was worth it and she needed to be kinder to herself. My wife would have laughed if she'd heard me. Physician heal thyself and all that.

> Melissa Asbury @MelissaAsbury
> The kindest thing anyone has ever done for me was a stranger helping me cross the London tube network with three children under 6.

Remember right at the start of this book when I said I was old-fashioned? Well, this is the kind of thing I'm talking about. Helping someone who is clearly struggling while just trying to get by. I avoid the Tube in London if I can because I find it horrifically claustrophobic. And I can't tell you how many men's crotches I've been faced with in my time. But when I do take the Tube or the bus I always offer to carry prams up the stairs or make sure a child is OK while their parent sorts themselves out. Remember also when I said I was often angry at the world? Well, this is one thing that really grinds my gears. Me, a tiny Scottish woman, helping lug a pram up the steep stairs of an Underground station while young men (and women) run past. What is so important? What means that you can't take two minutes to help someone out? Answer – nothing. Unless you are a transplant surgeon and you're late for an operation (in which case you should really think about your timekeeping) or there is an actual threat to life and limb you should stop and help someone out. And if you're a boss reading this, have a think. If your employee were ten minutes late for work because they had helped someone on the Tube, would you be upset? If you would, then have a bigger think. It could be someone you love who feels a rising tide of panic as they wonder if they can cope. Heck, one day it could be you. Kind bosses are the best bosses.

idk @thenextshell
In costa I mentioned that I couldn't afford a big drink and the barista overheard and brought me over a large anyway!

I love these tiny moments in time. They're memorable. That barista has cheered up a stranger and they've remembered it. I remember once I was in a coffee shop and they asked my name so they could shout it out when my drink was ready. For some reason I became annoyed at this, mainly because I'm terrifically grumpy (I did warn you), so I remembered my favourite scene from the film *Pulp Fiction* and, in my best Uma Thurman voice, said, 'Mrs Mia Wallace.' The barista didn't get the reference, wrote it on the cup and I carried on queuing. Shortly afterwards I heard the same member of staff ask the gentleman behind me what his name was, and he casually said, 'Vincent Vega.' I turned round and smiled at the man, he shrugged and we went on our way. But he saw I was trying to have some fun and he joined in. And it made my day.

Dame Julie Moore @CEOjuliem
When my friend's mother fell a stranger left work to drive her home.

I'm always concerned about older people. My parents are in vigorous health, but I do worry as they age about what might happen if they were taken ill or fell. They wouldn't consider themselves infirm, obviously, and if they read this book, they'd be horrified at me worrying, but I do. I appreciate little more than those who understand the vulnerability of the generation above us. I was on a Virgin train last year, and I was travelling first class because I'm fancy. An older woman got on and I smiled at her (I love smiling at people, even if they hate it). She smiled back but I immediately noticed that she had a giant boiled-egg-sized lump on her head that was clearly a new injury. I asked her if she was OK and she explained that she'd been running for the train and had fallen on the platform and hit her head. Community Action Susan stepped in at this point and I enlisted the help of the train crew, who were marvellous. A hot sweet tea appeared and some ice for her head. She was clearly upset though and I asked her why. She said it was because she only had a standard-class ticket and she was worried as she was sitting in first class. She got up to move and I was having none of it. I told her to stay where she was and that I would deal with the train manager. I got myself ready for a fight; you know what train conductors are like. They care about nothing but the money you've paid. The gentleman in charge appeared and I accosted him with the story. I told him I didn't want her to move and that I would pay the difference if he was going to be difficult about it. He smiled at me, checked the woman was OK and told her to sit where she was for the rest of her journey. He was amazing. When she reached her stop he personally came to escort her to the platform and had radioed ahead to make sure that a member of staff was there to take her to a taxi. I could have hugged him. I think I maybe did.

Marianne Skelcher @MarianneSkel
Scary looking young man who carried my heavy suitcase up steep stairs at Leeds station.#kindness

I love this tweet. A few pages ago I got really angry about young, strong people not helping others out and this young man did. I would love to have seen Marianne's face when the 'scary' young man finished his task.

CHAPTER 13

THE ANSWER IS **THE INTERNET**

I SHOULD KNOW, I GOOGLED IT

WHEN looking for a place to lay blame for the lack of kindness in life, the easiest place to look is, of course, the Internet. And I don't mean one should search the Internet for the answer; I mean the information superhighway is, itself, a soul-sapping joy vacuum. I had mused over whether to write this chapter because blaming social media and the Web is an easy option these days. There's very little that can't be laid at the door of our obsession with connectivity. Relationships don't last as long as they used to; that's because of jealousy caused by Facebook. Young people don't talk proper anymore; that's because of text-speak, which they all use. I can't buy Angel Delight in as many supermarkets anymore; that's because of pressure from the alt-right.

Let me start by saying that the Internet is, in many ways, a brilliant thing, not least because it's allowed many more people to find out a lot more stuff (whether important, silly or downright confusing) than they could before the advent of computers. Before the information superhighway enveloped society with a tsunami of funny animal pictures (you're welcome, by the way), access to information was a privilege of the elite and wealthy who kept great works of literature in their own homes. If you weren't rich enough to own your own copies of the great works of literature you might have had limited access in a currently ever-diminishing national treasure, the public library. I used to go to the library at Knightswood Community Centre with my gran. She would get a Mills and Boon and I would choose a book to enjoy in the summer holidays, when we spent most of our days scouring the shelves. I loved the library; it smelled of lavender and dentures. To my tiny self it seemed huge and filled with mysterious tomes that held the answer to all life's problems. It also helped that Knightswood Community Centre was the location of the single greatest triumph in my life and the first time in my life that I won anything. The 1982 Knightswood Community Centre Miniature Garden Competition. The premise was simple: you got a tea tray and turned it into a tiny garden. I took the affair very seriously and, using tin foil (for a pond), various vegetables (broccoli trees), and some of my Smurf accessories (plastic mushroom houses), I dazzled the judges with my eclectic interpretation of the brief.

The flipside to the avalanche of information provided by the Internet is that there are many people who will never experience the pleasure of a public library. The excitement of finding a title that you'd wanted to read. The fear when you didn't return it on time. In the same way that generations of young people will never know how it feels to wait a year to watch a film, queuing at

Azad Video just to get your hands on one of the two copies of *Ghostbusters 2* that were available to rent.

Because everyone now has the ability to find the answer to everything courtesy of their phone, the Internet is responsible for the growth in *teneo is totus*. That's 'know it all' in Latin. I googled it. Which is an example of what I'm talking about. I'm from the time when you couldn't just find the answer to a question by asking the hive mind. I got my first mobile phone in 1999, and before that the most technological invention I'd come across was something called a phonecard. In my first year as a trainee lawyer, all emails came to the partner in charge, who would print them out and put them in our in-tray.

The Internet has done much to increase the availability of information for those with a computer or a smartphone, but it's dumbed down many a conversation. The availability of information doesn't mean that people really understand what they've read, but what it does allow you to do is pretend to be more knowledgeable than you actually are, and look down on those who have large fingers and so can't type quickly. Even worse than intellectual snobbery is intellectual snobbery from people who don't understand what they're being snobbish about! Increasingly the phrase 'I'm just popping to the toilet' is simply code for 'I'm just popping to the toilet where I'll look up what we've been talking about, so I can pretend I always knew the answer and it's just come to me, and in doing so I will firmly establish that I'm the alpha male/female of the group.' It used to be OK to say that you didn't know the answer to something. It used to be OK for a group of people to discuss questions like 'Which is the oldest subway system in the world?' or 'What's the best way to make pancakes?' or 'When was "John Wayne Is Big Leggy" released?' The Internet means ignorance is no longer bliss.

The Freddie Mercury song 'The Great Pretender' should be the theme tune to society today. Of course I know about politics in the Middle East; I read about it on the *Huffington Post*. Sure, I've read Tolstoy. Well – I've seen the Tumblr. I'm guilty of it myself. My love of the television show *Casualty* coupled with medical websites means that I genuinely believe I have sufficient knowledge to operate on someone. If someone collapses now, I know what to say to make myself sound like a doctor: 'I need CBCs, chem 7, Us and Es and page X-ray – I need a chest and pelvis stat.' Bang. Now I'm a consultant. Anyone want to help me demonstrate? Just collapse. It'll be fine, honestly – I can perform a tracheotomy with a biro.

Access to limitless information allows people to intellectualise their thoughts without putting in the effort. And why would someone do that, you may ask? Simple. Because then you can elevate a simple thought into something that seems more classier because it seems more cleverer.

Take political comedy, an amorphous term in itself. Often conflated with satire, it's a term bandied about with gay abandon by journalists and commentators. I'm not one to hanker after 'the old days' where we all used to sit around the dinner table and discuss the contents of Hansard, but when you wanted to make a joke about a political party's policy you had to do a certain amount of research about it – you had to actually understand it.

Now you can google what you want and find out, in tiny sound bites, what you want to know.

What that means is that you can, if you want, be a political comic without ever knowing about politics. It's easy. Buzzwords work, quotes are good. For example, take comedy piñata Boris Johnson. Many jokes have been made about the Conservative politician, but how do you make a joke about him impressive to a comedy critic? How do you make a simple quip about him brainier, more intellectual, more good and that? Why not google 'Nietzsche quotes' and you can fit any of them to his life. 'Whoever fights monsters should see to it that in the process he does not become a monster. And if you gaze long enough into an abyss, the abyss will gaze back into you.' Add some of that to a simple statement and you get something like 'Boris Johnson's getting all Nietzsche on us. He's been staring into an abyss for a long time. Or, as I prefer to call it, the government's foreign policy.' Bang, now I'm a political comic.

The Internet makes people more confident about their opinions because there's always somewhere online with some evidence to back up their views. I can't tell you the number of times I've seen people angry about something that is simply not true or didn't happen. Or, conversely, screaming and demanding evidence of something that definitely did happen.

I genuinely don't remember the same amount of aggression in discourse when I was growing up. I look back with fondness on those halcyon days before we got caught in the Web. I got my first email address in 1996 when I was at university, around the time they opened something called a 'computer lab'. Imagine the technology! I didn't have a mobile phone, or Facebook or Twitter (and I survived quite nicely), and to be honest I wasn't entirely sure how this Internet thing worked but it seemed quite useful. When writing my dissertation about defamation it meant that I could access cases and articles that previously would have been unavailable to me, and it also meant that essays didn't need to be written longhand anymore, which was a bonus for my lecturers. I like to think of my handwriting as eccentric and florid; others would say it was impenetrable and horrific. If I got a bad grade for an essay I would always dismiss it as being the result of the fact my 's's look like 'b's. Which doesn't help when the topic is 'Systemic solutions to social care standards'.

At that point, though, the technology was useful for very low-level things, like looking at pictures of Jodie Foster. I didn't really email anyone; I didn't quite understand message boards, and the majority of people I knew didn't have access to the World Wide Web. Even when I started work in the late 1990s it still wasn't commonplace to have access to the Internet. We most certainly didn't have the ability to go online – but to be honest we didn't know we wanted to.

Nowadays my phone is my connection to the world. Emails are responded to within five minutes, articles sent and read immediately and gossip spread within seconds. Back then it was different. My mobile phone at the turn of the millennium only stored about five text messages and they cost so much to send I'd rather use a payphone.

Most importantly, I didn't know that people needed to know what was inside my head. Thoughts were kept relatively private and we carried on with life as if that was absolutely fine. Today it's not so simple. Today we can find out what people think whether we want to or not and thoughts can be expressed from behind a veil of false identities and troll accounts. Although not everyone feels the need to hide behind anonymity. As I was writing this book I saw the latest tweet from the president of the United States.

> 'Crazy Joe Biden is trying to act like a tough guy. Actually, he is weak, both mentally and physically, and yet he threatens me, for the second time, with physical assault. He doesn't know me, but he would go down fast and hard, crying all the way. Don't threaten people Joe!'

That's the president threatening someone. Which is why, when people talk about regulating social media platforms, I despair. They're not going to be regulated; they're always going to be full of people tweeting and posting nasty things because that's what they're for. Twitter is made for aggression. Very few characters and the immediacy of posting means that it is, in essence, a very public shouting match.

I've written about social media in the past and my opinion of it hasn't changed. I think it's a marvellous thing, which is often ruined by a small number of people who want to use it for negative purposes. I enjoy Twitter and Facebook and have made genuine friends from interactions that I've had on there. Replies on Twitter are like the unfiltered psyche of the nation and the months I spent dancing proved that beyond a doubt.

I don't know whether social media causes aggression or whether it just provides a platform for it, but in a way the cause of the negativity is irrelevant. It's there for everyone to see. There's a strange attitude amongst some that if you're on Twitter you can say what you want to anyone. That if someone has a Twitter account that means they're fair game to have any old crap lobbed at them for no reason whatsoever. Freedom of speech as a concept would support that, and indeed I believe that people should have the right to express themselves. But having the option or power to say something is different from actually doing it. I've thought many negative things about many people but haven't felt the need to express those thoughts, and certainly not to them directly. I often wonder when people stopped thinking about that difference; that having an opinion is fine but expressing it to someone would be cruel.

I know that I'm not the slimmest person but it always made me laugh when I was called fat. As if it was the first time it had ever occurred to someone. But I would never in a million years comment on a friend's weight, never mind a stranger's. Because it's personal and hurtful. I got endless tweets about how I look like Wee Jimmy Krankie, which is not, for information, an original thought. Those sniggering at their keyboards mean it as an insult but those people probably never watched Janette Krankie in panto and so have missed out on one of the greatest comic performances you'll see on stage. I take it as a compliment.

Such comparisons, meant to cause distress, often reveal

a great deal about the insulter. When I'm compared to someone else it's clear that they don't rate me, but they also don't rate the other person. It's a double insult, if you will. As I say, I don't think it's an insult to be compared to a Krankie, but some do. I got increasingly angry in the week that I dressed as Daenerys Targaryen on *Strictly*, because people kept tweeting me that I looked like Gemma Collins from *TOWIE*. I'm not upset about the comparison – I've never watched her before or met the woman – but I knew it wasn't kind to either of us.

Freedom of speech is a wonderful thing. Without it we wouldn't have experienced the political and social change that makes us who we are. We need to be able to express what we believe and through the power of our words change the world. You can say whatever you want, but in my view, kindness means that sometimes you shouldn't.

One of my favourite tweets that I received when I first started on *Strictly* was – and I'm paraphrasing here – 'So they let pigs dance now?' I replied, 'No, but they do let dicks on Twitter.'

At what point did we dehumanise people so much that their feelings don't count? On more than one occasion when I replied to someone being cruel I was told that I'd put myself on television, so I should damn well take whatever anyone wanted to say. Is that how it works now? Decency and kindness stop when you're in the public eye? The price of 'fame' is constant abuse and negativity? Very few people, even celebrities, don't feel something when they're attacked like this.

I got away lightly on social media compared to some

of my fellow contestants. The vitriol and abuse levelled at people who were, in essence, simply dancing on a Saturday night was extraordinary. I felt angrier for them than I did for myself. To see some of the things that people sent to my fellow contestants made me incandescent with rage. What on earth has happened to us that from the safety of a computer screen we think we can scream abuse at a fellow human being?

We all respond differently to such situations, and I've spent many a night worrying about whether I should reply to someone or just leave it be. I remember, when I received some random bit of abuse on Twitter about my performance or the way that I looked, I replied. The fact that I responded seemed to upset some people. Firstly, because if I did I would attract others to insult the person who initially insulted me, and that wasn't fair to them. What a marvellous argument. Shout at me all you like but heaven forbid I actually respond. Maybe it's because people don't think I do my own social media. I do, you know. It's me, sitting in my pants, posting pictures of cats at three in the morning. Oh, the glamour!

The second and most intriguing reason why I was told I shouldn't reply to abusers on social media was that I had put myself in the public eye so I somehow deserved it. How curious. For a start I didn't 'put myself in the public eye'; I wanted to be a comedian. And even if someone is famous just for being famous they are still a human being.

In the same way that you can catch an HTD from someone, spending time on social media can have the opposite effect. I've become angry from spending five minutes scrolling through my Twitter feed. It's stupid. If something else made me feel that way I would avoid it. For example, I dislike jam. I'd even go so far as to say that I hate jam. If you have a visceral reaction to that statement, you're not alone. Many times I've found myself confronted by an angry baker who can't understand why the thought of a sugary fruit concoction gives me the dry boke but it does. (For information, the word 'boke' means vomit, and so 'the dry boke' is the act of gagging without actually being sick. It's a Scottish idiom that I love, and so by explaining it I'm hoping my editor may let it remain in the book. Use it liberally. It's my gift to you.)

My aversion to jam actually makes life very difficult. Birthday cakes, doughnuts, biscuits are all slathered with it because of the incorrect assumption that everyone likes jam. Some of us don't. See also marmalade, chocolate spread and meat paste. And don't get me started on marzipan – I'll lash out. I hate them. They make me angry. Anyway – back to my analogy . . . I wouldn't spend fifteen minutes in the morning sobbing while licking apricot jam from a spoon, would I? Why the hell do I spend my time reading the thoughts of angry people?

And that's one of the most difficult aspects of the Internet, because it drives a dagger through the very heart of this book. I want everyone to love each other and be kind and respectful, but you know what? Some people are just dicks. The elephant in this room is that a lot of people hate each other and express that hatred freely. Just recently I tweeted about *Cheer Up Love* and suggested that people might want to read a cheerful book about depression. I received this reply:

> @SusanCalman I wouldn't bother. Nothing depresses me more than an inept, dyke dwarf. Absolutely fuckin' useless

I reported the person who sent it, and it turned out he was responsible for a number of other homophobic communications, so the sad truth is that he appears to hate me because I'm gay. I don't think, whatever attempts are made at reconciliation, even Isambard Kingdom Brunel could ever build a bridge with that person.

This is a tough quandary for me. The book is about kindness and joy and listening to people and ending conflict with hugs. But is there a point where even the kindest of people would throw their hands up in despair and walk away? It pains me to say it but yes, there are some people who even I, with my message of positivity, should be kept away from.

My wife has a lot of say in what I do in my career. I have some input of course, but she knows me better than anyone else and she is also aware that there are certain situations where I would struggle to keep control. While a lot of this book is full of wishy-washy lefty love-and-hugs nonsense, I'm not that controlled in real life. I have a terrible temper and can fly off the handle at very little notice. I've worked hard to control it because it's not very in keeping with my new positive life, and no one needs to see that nice lady from the dancing show screaming her head off in the middle of the street at a pigeon that got in her way. My temper is the thing I hate most about myself and I have the self-awareness to know for a fact that there are some people who would push all my buttons. That would not be good. And if it were filmed it would be awful.

As a result of this personality quirk, I am banned from doing certain shows. Not by the television companies (although I am always suspicious about why, despite my best efforts, I've never been allowed to guest present the *Six O'Clock News* – I would be brilliant at it; I even practise my little 'goodbye' smile for the end-link), but by my wife, who has told me I am definitely not allowed to take part in *I'm a Celebrity . . . Get Me Out of Here!* because either the toilets or my fellow campmates would make me lose it. Also *Big Brother*. The casting of these types of shows is often deliberately confrontational, and I'd probably be stuck in the *Big Brother* house with a misogynist homophobe and, despite being filmed twenty-four hours a day and knowing that I should be polite, would find it difficult to hold my tongue. It would end with me screaming blue murder at a fascist and I would end up as the mad bitch who lost it on prime-time television. I am most certainly not allowed to do *Dancing on Ice*. But that's less to do with my temper and more to do with the fact I am desperately clumsy and would probably kill myself live on television. What a way to go. I am allowed to do *MasterChef*, though, because no one looks like a dick on *MasterChef*. Although I'm always happy to be a trailblazer.

My point is I get the fact that there are some people who we just can't see ourselves sitting down with and having a conversation. More than that, there are many people who I don't think would change their minds even if faced with the most rational arguments in the world. But it's easy to give up on an idea because of the worst-case scenario. I couldn't imagine having a cup of tea and a chat with members of a political party who supported racist policies. I struggle to think how I could politely converse with those who seek to restrict women's rights or who object to LGBTQ equality, but they are the extremes and their intransigence shouldn't stop us from trying to communicate.

I struggle so much to find any form of solution to the aggression and combative nature of the Internet. To the rapidly increasing gulf between us all. The problem is that if we all stay in our camps and never reach out to others, we simply become more entrenched in our own perspective. Can we believe that, as the wonderful Jo Cox said, 'We are far more united and have far more in common with each other than things that divide us.' Because she's right. The trouble is, sometimes I read things so offensive, so hurtful, that I cannot believe I'm from the same species as the people who've said them.

Setting aside those who commit a criminal act with hate speech or some other offence, who would deservedly be reported to Twitter and the relevant authorities, if someone espouses unspeakable views on Twitter I, personally, tend to block them. I know that many would suggest that that's not the way to deal with it and letting them know that they've upset me is exactly what they want, but I like to know that they can't see what I'm doing. They don't deserve my happy pictures. Some of my friends take on the trolls and I've always been slightly in awe of people who do that. I don't think I'm consistently strong enough for it. I'm happy to debate with someone sitting in the same room as me but there's something quite uncomfortable about exchanging sound bites with someone who may not even be using their real name.

I'm not one for using inspirational quotes for guidance but during the infamous presidential campaign in which Trump was triumphant, Michelle Obama's rousing speech where she declared, 'When they go low, we go high' captures what I wish I could say. Even when people are being downright rude to me I try my best to respond politely. One of the best tweets I ever received simply said,

'Fuck off Calman'

I responded:

'Thanks! Remember to vote on Saturday night!'

I hope that made the person who sent it to me angry. It would make me feel amazing if someone, somewhere was furious that I was polite. The Internet, by its very being, gives an outlet to those who seek to promote negativity and hatred. It doesn't provide a level playing field for those who seek the opposite. I don't always manage it, but I try to respond with politeness and courtesy even to the most inappropriate of tweets. I hope that by not being dragged into their way of corresponding I can take the high road. It's not that their opinions don't make me angry, it's not that I don't want to change their minds and challenge them, it's just that I know my own limitations. I know that if I go down that rabbit hole of kindness and start screaming at them, I'll become them. Insults are easy; I'm a comedian after all. I deal with hecklers all the time. I can make a grown man cry if I want to. But the point is, I don't want to.

There's an amazing programme on television called *The Curse of Oak Island*. Two brothers have spent millions of dollars and years of their life trying to find treasure on a small island off the coast of Nova Scotia. It's addictive viewing. Every week the voiceover breathlessly narrates something like 'Will they find the Ark of the Covenant? Is it possible that Shakespeare's manuscripts were buried hundreds of feet underground? Is this the very spot where the Knights Templar hid some of the greatest and most valuable artefacts known to man?' There's never an answer. They just keep digging. And that's what social media is for me: there's no clear answer, we just keep plodding onwards, taking the good and trying to find a way to deal with the bad. I know that at some point I might not be able to continue to do my own Twitter and Facebook, but I'll resist it as long as possible. I like communicating with the world from my desk at six in the morning. I think the majority of people who inhabit the strange cyberworld are good and decent. The negative aspects of it don't need to be the legacy of our time there.

I treat social media like it's afternoon tea. I'm a scone and I'm often offered jam (trolls) or cream (people posting funny GIFs of pandas sneezing). If someone offers me jam to add to my baked goods I politely decline and ask for cream instead. And that's what I do. I have more cream. It's lovely.

CHAPTER 14
COMMUNITY ACTION
CALMAN
YOU WANT HER ON YOUR SIDE

KINDNESS and joy are like chocolate fondue. Excellent if enjoyed by yourself but even better when friends stick their faces in it. Thinking of ourselves as solo warriors in a fight to survive doesn't make the world a better place. It makes it cold and lonely. Community is vitally important in my crusade, and is the key to spreading kindness and joy. It's a concept that can scare some people, though. It raises questions like, do we know our neighbours? Do we want to get to know them? Or is it better to shut the door when you come home and not make any contact with people around you? Can I get specially trained guard sharks with lasers attached to their heads to swim around a moat I've dug myself? Perhaps not. I don't think my insurance covers me if the postman is eaten, even if I have clearly posted warning signs.

Lots of things in this world frighten me. Planes, trains, automobiles, clogs and even raisins. But the thing that frightens me most of all is loneliness. I've been desperately lonely in my life before and I spent most of my time from my teens to my mid-twenties trying to make contact with other human beings. I was working, I had friends, but I felt completely alone. I don't think anything has sucked the joy from my soul like it. I'm frightened of it returning, of finding myself back in that dark, bad place. I think that's why I am so determined to not be alone, to find connections with people any way I can. Community, whether online or in real life, is absolutely crucial in my mission. Not only can you find joy, you can share it.

I've been concerned with the concept of neighbourhood and commonality for many years, but it's recently been brought into sharp focus. Because I've bought a house. A proper, grown-up house. Believe me when I say that I don't mean to brag about my change in living arrangements; I bought the house for one simple reason. Donald Trump. My wife and I have always been tremendously financially frugal and never spend outside our means, but as soon as Mr Trump was elected president we thought, 'Well if we're going to die, we may as well die in the big house.' So, we went to the bank and had the following conversation:

Me: Can we have an unfeasibly large mortgage please?

Bank Manager: Can you pay it back?

Me: Does it really matter anymore?

Bank Manager: Not really.

And that's why I bank with the Royal Bank of Scotland. After a lot of admin and some unsavoury begging to a nice lady in charge of loans, we bought a house and it is quite a change. For most of my adult life I'd lived in flats, so having an upstairs and a downstairs was one of the most thrilling things I've ever encountered. For a start it makes sulking better. It was always a bit of a pain when living in a small apartment to have an argument and then storm off, only to go as far as the hallway before standing for ten minutes, furious, and then having to slope back into the living room. It never had the drama that I think a proper strop requires. Whereas now I can storm up the stairs and sit in a huff for hours before my wife apologises for whatever she has done. Or I get hungry.

Having two floors to live on makes me feel like a million bucks. And I tell you, nothing makes you feel more like an adult than hoovering the stairs. I mean I haven't done it yet, but when I do it will feel amazing. I also have a thermostat for the first time. It's electronic. I love it. If you'd told me at the age of sixteen that at the age of forty-three I would have an Excel spreadsheet of the ambient temperature of my house I would say you were a liar. It's my life now. Did you know that there is a Facebook group for people who like their thermostats more than their families? I joined it. Those people are fabulous.

I lived in a flat for fifteen years and while I knew and liked my neighbours we weren't that close. It was partly due to the nature of the accommodation – there were no shared spaces or gardens that we would sit in of an after- noon and shoot the breeze. It didn't help that the majority of those in my block had young families, and there's only so many times I can pretend to enjoy spending time with

Susan Calman

screaming young people. But we knew everyone, got on with them; indeed, many of them came to our wedding. My neighbour would bring food for Lee when I was away for long periods of time as a gesture of friendship and kindness and we would take rubbish out for the older tenants. I know for a fact that some people in the street were slightly frightened of how much attention I paid to the local area. For example, rubbish was a terrible problem in the street. Either people would dump refuse on the pavement and leave it for the foxes to destroy and spread far and wide, or vans would arrive and empty their cargo of building rubble, washing machines and various items that they didn't want to take to the tip.

It would drive me mad in the mornings when I left the house to see food and waste strewn across the street. So, I took matters into my own hands. I laminated signs and tied them to lampposts asking people not to dump rubbish and reminding them of the council's regulations. I went out and swept the pavements to keep them clean. Once I even found myself chasing after a white van that had dumped a magnificent load of stuff (under the 'no fly-tipping' sign), screaming, 'I've got your number plate, I will find you!' My wife hilariously gave me the nickname Community Action Barbie, which only made me happier about my self-appointed role as street litter warden. You might be reading this and rolling your eyes. What a busybody! What a pain in the arse! And I'm sure many of my neighbours would sigh as they saw me, in my pyjamas, sweeping up broken glass or Sellotaping another homemade sign to a door. But I don't care.

Nothing will stop me trying to make wherever I live a better place.

With my record for interfering in village affairs, when we moved to our new house we were, understandably, nervous. This was our forever home, and I'm sure I'm not alone in watching countless documentaries on nightmare neighbours, so prior to moving day I lay awake at night worrying about what we were going to encounter. We moved in on a wet December night to a house that had lain empty for several months, was cold, smelled more than a little bit odd and needed substantial renovation. A problem with contracts of sale and purchase meant that the move itself was frantic and rushed and pretty tense. Eventually payment was exchanged at five in the afternoon, the removal trucks sped to the house, we chucked everything that we'd ever owned into the hallway and shut the door. The first night we arrived I shed quite a few tears. What had we done? We'd moved from our cosy flat where we knew everyone to a street of strangers. The first full day in the new house was spent attempting to unpack. The mess was horrendous, the size of the task almost overwhelming. My wife and I changed into our pyjamas at 5 p.m. and sat on the sofa surrounded by boxes and rubbish. That was when the doorbell went for the first time. Two doors up just wanted to drop a card and some flowers in to welcome us. Then someone else arrived from three doors up. They wanted to say hello as well and if we needed anything just to shout. Next door on the left dropped in the bin schedule and let us know about the drains (dodgy at times). Next door on the right waved and came in for a cup of tea. Next door two up followed after that and then the people at the top of the street gave us an extra bin (which is worth its weight in gold). Before the end of the week we knew everyone, and everyone knew us. That first Christmas we had a drinks party in our house and our neighbours sat, in an unfinished and rather uncomfortable house, on the one piece of furniture we had, politely eating snacks made in a malfunctioning oven. I knew from that first week that I would love where I was living because we immediately felt part of the street and the kindness shown towards us was delightful.

Some of my friends refuse to speak to their neighbours. They see it as an intrusion into their privacy to feel forced to converse with strangers who they just happen to be living beside. I understand that, I absolutely do. But I love feeling part of a community, of caring for people and taking pride in where I live. In the recent heavy snow, we borrowed shovels from each other and gritted paths. We texted neighbours who might have trouble leaving the house to make sure they were OK. I walked to the super-market for provisions and distributed them like a tiny missionary. My next-door neighbours, Pamela and Rodger, left a bottle of wine on the adjoining wall so that we could have a drink to get us through snowmaggedon and it turned into a rather lovely time when the street came together to make sure everyone got through unscathed.

Disappointingly, I haven't had to chase after a single van yet. The most community action that this Barbie has seen is screaming at a man who emptied the rubbish from his car directly onto the pavement outside my house. I threw open the window and yelled obscenities at him. Then I shut my window and realised that I'd turned into my mother. I always promised myself when I was a youngster that that would never happen to me. Not because she's a bad person – she's utterly lovely – but because it would mean I was old. Because in my head I would be forever young, and unlike the older generation I would never criticise young people for what they wore or what they said. I would live the revolution forever! Sadly, turning into my parents seems as inevitable as Christmas.

For example, last week I was in the pub. It's an old-fashioned establishment with small facilities comprising two cubicles and a small sink. I entered with the determination of a woman who has foolishly held on until the last minute to go to relieve herself. In what can only be described as a nightmare scenario, both cubicles were engaged and I could hear coming from behind each of the doors two women rather drunkenly chatting about boys and stuff. In such a situation you tend to get a sixth sense for how long they will be in there – is the conversation coming to a close or are they, as in this story, only halfway through a marathon discussion about whether their respective partners are good enough for them? Spoiler alert: no they're not. I tried to be patient, I really did, but it was approaching a crisis situation and one of the most awkward parts of being on *Strictly* was that I knew if I had an accident a video of the ensuing chaos would be on Twitter quicker than I could say, 'Spare trousers'. It was at that point I heard myself shouting, loudly and in a voice that I recognise from my teenage years, 'I'm sure

Susan Calman

you're all having a lovely time in there, but these are toilets and some of us have to use them.' The patrons stumbled out of the cubicles mumbling apologies and I found myself remarking, 'It's not just you in here, you know.'

But I digress. Community may be an old-fashioned notion and I'm pretty sure that a decent argument could be made that it no longer exists. But it can carry on if we want it to. I know that there are practical difficulties in our way. People used to put down roots earlier in life, stay in the same place and have a job for life: all things that don't apply as much now. People move home and careers far more than a few decades ago. It means that those lifelong connections are rarer than before, but they're still not impossible to make.

I like being part of a community, of many communities. The gorgeous RuPaul once said, 'We as gay people get to choose our family and the people we're around. I am your family. We are a family here.' I think as people we get to choose our community and make it what we want it to be. I find that caring about where I live makes me kinder and it certainly makes me happier.

In the summer there's a fair in the local park. It's not like walking into Alton Towers by any means, but there are stalls and a raffle. I won a tiny bottle of booze in the tombola, which I prize to this day. I met new people and saw friends who I hadn't spoken to in a while and the day left me with an immense feeling of pride that where I lived we cared about each other.

I don't want anyone to be lonely. I know what that's like. But if you've not yet found the people who you want to surround yourself with, maybe you can start it off. Choose the community that you want to live in – reach out, whether it's next door or down the street. It's a frightening thing to do but it's also beautiful when it works.

Build it and they will come.

CHAPTER 15
YOU DON'T KNOW ME
KINDNESS IS INDIVIDUALITY

KINDNESS takes many forms, and one of the most important is allowing human beings to be the fragile, glorious, changeable idiots that we are. One of my favourite television shows is *The West Wing*, which, although somewhat dated, is something I return to again and again. Especially after watching the current American president tweet, well, anything that comes into his head. The series details the ups and downs of the White House and the fictional president Josiah Bartlet. In the earlier episodes, West Wing staff are struggling with the fact that the man they helped get elected isn't doing what they thought he would. After much rumination and concern they come up with the solution, and it's very simple: 'Let Bartlet be Bartlet'.

It's a gloriously concise mantra that I've used myself on numerous occasions. Even on *Strictly*, where I fully embraced the dresses and the wigs, I realised that I had a line and I would not cross it. False nails. I hated those things. Oddly enough it was the application of those talons that made me more uncomfortable than anything else I was asked to do. The aesthetic problem is that I bite my nails and so, to the incredibly talented and caring people in make-up, the sight of my nibbled digits was no doubt an affront to humanity. I calmly explained to them that I couldn't function with false nails on, that they made me feel awful. One last time they asked me why I didn't want to take the final step towards glamour. I looked at them, smiled and said, 'Let Calman be Calman.' If the television audience were sick on themselves seeing the reality of my fingers, then so be it. I needed to be myself. Whatever that meant.

Kindness also means letting people be who they are even if we don't know what that is. I've rarely encountered anyone I've interviewed as part of my job who, when I've said, 'Tell me about yourself,' has answered either fully or truthfully. Because we change and evolve, we are different things to different people, we're individuals. Trying to define an individual human being is as pointless as a phone-in discussion on whether or not people should use phones. Being defined and put in boxes is limiting. We're not always what we seem and that's brilliant. Little makes me more annoyed than when people judge me without knowing who I am.

One afternoon a few years ago, my mum and I were in town and decided to pop into a posh ladies' boutique. Of course, we weren't going to buy anything – I find any shop that only sells clothes in single-figure sizes doesn't tend to fit my sense of style (or waistline) – but there's nothing like looking at a suit that costs the same as my

monthly mortgage payment to cheer me up. But our enjoyment was hampered after about five minutes when we
realised that we were being followed round the shop by
a burly, and quite conspicuous, security guard. We'd clearly
been identified as potential shoplifters, although I'm not
sure why we looked so suspicious. I'd deliberately left my
bag with 'swag' embroidered on it at home. I became
increasingly angry about the situation and as we made
our way to the exit I turned to give the man a piece of
my mind. But my mum, a normally placid woman, placed
her hand on my arm, turned to the guard, patted her
handbag and said, with utter confidence:

'Big mistake. Big. Huge.'

I'm not sure what was more surprising: that my mother
had the confidence to confront a man who looked like
Vin Diesel, or the fact that she'd seen *Pretty Woman*. And
apparently memorised it. I resolved to use the same tactic
if a similar situation arose again. Luckily, I didn't have to
wait long.

I was travelling by train recently and decided to treat
myself by purchasing a first-class ticket. I wouldn't
normally splash out on such an extravagance because it
was a short journey, but the train was packed to the brim
with unhappy commuters. It's an uncomfortable situation
at the best of times but it's made even worse for me because
of my short stature. When on public transport I either
find myself face to crotch with a sweating passenger or
left with mild concussion when a tall person turns around
and smashes me in the face with a rucksack.

I got on the train and stepped into the VIP area. Already

seated were three besuited businessmen and, perched on the edge of one of the tables, was the conductor. He stood up as soon as I entered, moved forward, looked me up and down and said, with a smirk, 'You do know that you need to have a first-class ticket to sit here.'

I knew what he was insinuating; like the security guard in the shop, he was judging me, unfavourably, on how I looked. But instead of getting annoyed I remembered my mother, channelling the spirit of Julia Roberts and kicking ass. I pulled myself up to my full height, looked up into his eyes, gave him my best Paddington Bear stare and said, quite calmly, 'Don't I look like a first-class type of lady? What class of lady do you think I am?' The conductor's smile faded a little. I produced my ticket, held it up to his face and calmly sat down. He stopped smiling altogether. I think he'd hoped that I would scuttle away to sit with the riff-raff in standard class, leaving the travelling Bullingdon Club to remain unmolested by the great unwashed. I smiled the whole way home.

I'm sure many of you reading this will have encountered similar displays of snobbery. And it's easy when it happens to let it irritate the hell out of you. Now I take a leaf out of my mum's book. In fact, I'm looking forward to my next encounter with a snob. I'm Susan Calman playing Julia Roberts playing a hooker with a heart and I deserve an Oscar.

Speaking of which, I should really stop going shopping. It never ends well. I was in London with my wife and we decided to pop into Tiffany & Co. She had bought me a watch as a wedding present and I wanted to buy her one in return. That makes me sound totally lovely but actually I had an ulterior motive. My wife doesn't wear and has never worn a watch and it makes me physically sick. I live my life according to a precise timetable where I know exactly where I'm meant to be at every hour of every day. She sometimes doesn't know what day of the week it is. I used to ask her, 'What's the time?' even though I knew the time, to subtly tell her we were late for something. Every time I asked her she would shrug and smile and point at her wrist as if to say, 'I don't know, I'm not constrained by time, I don't have a watch.'

So, I thought I'd wrap a passive-aggressive point (she's a lucky lady) about her tardiness into the gift of a lovely timepiece, meaning she couldn't say no. We went into Tiffany dressed casually. We were by no means scruffy, but perhaps less posh than some of their customers. As we browsed we noticed a man following us. As we know, this had happened to me before, and this time I was determined to make an immediate point. I strode to the display case where the watches were laid out and said, very loudly, 'Which one do you want, darling?' My wife, having also noticed the security presence, pointed to one and said, 'That one!'

We didn't look at the price because we were determined to prove to the people in Tiffany that we could afford to be in that store and their preconceptions about us were damn well wrong. As the shop assistant scanned the barcode I whispered very gently to my wife, 'How much is it?' She indicated with her fingers the amount and I quickly calculated in my head if my credit card could cover the cost. It could, and even though it was much more than we wanted to spend, we bought the watch and walked proudly out of the shop like two toffs on holiday in Monte Carlo. That watch now sits proudly in a drawer at home because it doesn't matter how much money I spend, my wife still refuses to live life according to a timetable. She's an idiot.

Obviously these are personal experiences and all of you will have your own examples of irksome events. Of the type of annoyances and judgements that fill us with rage. People are quick to make assumptions, to categorise, to decide who we are and what we are without delving deeper into the reality of our lives. Perhaps if we had a more holistic approach to humanity we would all be happier.

We all make judgements based on how people look, how they sound, what they say, who they vote for, who they sleep with. But no one part of us defines what we are. The best example of what we're moving towards is what I call The Spice Girls definition of life. You're the sporty one, you're the posh one, you're the scary one, etc, etc. It's a good marketing tool but it's not real life. Being easy to define isn't always a good thing. Not knowing what to expect from someone can be scary but trying to judge people means that we miss out on connections. 'I won't like him, he voted for the Tories/Labour/Lib Dems.' Maybe you would. Maybe that's just one aspect of the person and the rest of them will be fabulous.

We are, as humans, full of delightful contradictions. The angry-looking man who saves kittens. The short lesbian who wants to wear a dress and dance with a man.

The next time you look at someone and judge them, why not take a deep breath and think. Do you know who they are or do you just think you do? Have you bothered to get to know them at all? Is part of your fear of a stranger that you don't know anything about them? For many years the scare stories spread about gay people came entirely from ignorance. We were all perverts and paedophiles and our sole aim was to corrupt the nation's children through the music of Frankie Goes to Hollywood. That's not who we were or are. Only when people started to think for themselves, and ignore the propaganda, did they realise how wrong those preconceptions were.

If we are kind to each other not only can we learn more but we can become less frightened of those who we consider different. Kindness is letting people change. Kindness is getting to know people. Kindness is letting people be people.

Let Calman be Calman. Let you be you.

CHAPTER 16
IT'S COOL TO BE KIND:

I BET JAMES DEAN HELPED PEOPLE WITH THEIR HEAVY SHOPPING

HOW do I persuade you, as this book trundles along, that being kind is the best possible way to live your life? I could bribe you, but I'll be honest – I'm not in the best place for that. I have a pot of change by my front door but there are a lot of old pound coins in it that I didn't manage to spend before the deadline and I don't think you'd want any of them, would you? Besides, paying people to do something would feel like it was a job and I want your kindness to come from a place of love and to be spontaneous and empowering. It has to be your decision and not one forced upon you. So perhaps I can try, in a rather ham-fisted way, to persuade you that being kind is cool.

I've always wanted, more than anything, to be cool. I blame the Brat Pack movies of the 1980s and more specifically Molly Ringwald. She was the epitome of cool. I wanted to be her more than anything else in the world and imagined myself with a homemade prom dress and quirky friends. I wasn't Molly Ringwald though. I was Susan Calman, I had a dress from Laura Ashley and my friends were as dull as I was. My entire life has been an attempt to live like I'm in *St Elmo's Fire*, and when I started stand-up all I wanted was to write and perform comedy shows that made people gasp and cry and vomit. Shows that newspaper arts critics would line up to review and that would win awards and plaudits. I'd wander along in a black polo neck and sunglasses looking really pissed off at things all the time, occasionally swearing at children, but people would forgive me because I'd be cool.

It doesn't take a trained psychologist to know why I want to be like this. It's school. Let's face it, it's always school. I was never cool when I was younger, and I always wanted to be. But that desire is, in truth, stupid. I don't want to perform my one-woman play about the Anti-Corn-Law League to twelve people in a basement in Shoreditch. I want to play to hundreds of people and make them laugh.

Oddly enough it's one thing that my dance boyfriend Kevin and I used to discuss at length. We'd both wanted to be the cool kids at school but never were. We spent hours imagining the dark, edgy productions we could put on together in order to be seen as the bad boys of comedy and dance. We would take over the world with our new form of entertainment. Who cares if only three people saw us; we could make our mark by people not wanting to see us. We'd spend our nights in clubs punching paparazzi and snogging reality TV stars while Instagramming pictures of champagne and cocaine. Surely that would make us the coolest cats in town. The thing was that that kind of show, that kind of image and that kind of person just wasn't us.

What was very clear about our time on *Strictly* was how many people appreciated the fact that two quite nice people were trying their best to dance without being idiots about it. Without question the fact there was no possibility of any hanky-panky between us helped. The '*Strictly* Curse' wasn't about to hit us. I'll never forget Kevin's sad wee face when I said to him at the start of our training that he was a lovely handsome man but there was absolutely no way I would ever find him attractive or want to sleep with him. Bless.

I would never consider myself a role model for anyone, but I know that I am. Lots of young people watch *Strictly Come Dancing* and my CBBC shows and to them I am someone to look up to. Is it so bad that I'm quite hard-working, happily married, have set up a pension and spend a lot of time rescuing animals? Kevin is a polite, kind, handsome man who doesn't have a problem with a really pushy, demanding lesbian telling him what to do. Yes, some would call us dull and we will never set the world alight with our showbiz lifestyle but maybe that's OK. Maybe, just maybe, dull people are actually rather cool.

Perhaps part of the problem regarding our attitude to kindness and the creeping destruction of joy are the people who we aspire to be now. Who and what is considered 'cool'. We're all influenced by the role models we're exposed to when we're growing up and what people are famous for now can be so negative. Becoming known for being rude and obnoxious and hateful can encourage those with an easily moulded mind to do the same. Negativity sells far better than positivity in many ways. And it's easier.

A newspaper column about how amazing everything is won't attract as many clicks as one full of gossip and innuendo. It was only when I was in the middle of something that the press were so interested in that I realised just how deep their desire for controversy, as opposed to normality, was.

I'd never really had much experience of these sorts of clickbait articles until I started on *Strictly*. Initially I'm not sure anyone really knew who I was, or more importantly what I was. I suppose I didn't make it easy for them. I wasn't the type of person one might expect to be on the show. I was a gay woman from Scotland, who still lived there, was married, a bit depressed, liked cats. I was on the radio a lot, but most people wouldn't know who I was, and I didn't really do anything interesting. The gay thing was really going to get in the way of any shagging stories that they would want to run unless the show was going to dance me straight. Imagine that: gay for forty-three years until I started to paso doble. There was a slight flurry of interest when my name was announced but it became clear from the very beginning that I wasn't particularly noteworthy when it came to the tabloids.

My first ever appearance in a celeb column was at the initial rehearsals for the show. My friend texted me and said my photo was in the paper and sent me a copy. It was me, walking along beside one of the producers of the show, and the caption read: 'Susan Calman and her assistant walk to rehearsals'. I laughed and laughed. The idea that I would have an assistant of any kind was a delight. Perhaps that's what you did when you became a bona fide celeb? I immediately looked into the legal situation if I hired one of my cats to fulfil such a role but was informed that if I had employees I would be responsible for their pensions. I don't have time for such things. But I carried on thinking that this kind of nonsense would all die down once the show started. Far from it. It only got worse.

The press interest was most obvious to me every Friday and Saturday when we stayed at the hotel before the live show at the weekend. The show put us up in an establishment near to the studio so that we could be ferried back and forward easily to make it for rehearsals and the like. The first time I arrived I was shocked at the crowd of photographers standing outside, snapping away. I had never, in all my life, been in that kind of situation. If any of those pictures still exist they are of a small frightened woman standing, like a meerkat, startled by the light. Those photographers were there every morning and evening when we returned to the hotel but as the weeks progressed I noticed something curious. They never took my picture. It was clear that in order to sell the product to the papers they had to have someone in them that the papers thought people wanted to see, and that was most certainly not me. It became something of a sport for me to see if I could, in any way, get into any of the shots. I would pop out from behind Debbie McGee; I'd hide behind the bins and then walk right in front of Aston Merrygold. I asked Gemma Atkinson once if she would mind if I snogged her as we got in the car to see if that might work. We didn't do it though as the headline would probably have read: 'Gemma Atkinson snogs mystery brunette'.

I'm not moaning about my lack of column inches – far from it; I enjoy the anonymity I'm afforded by people not caring – but what was intriguing was why I wasn't interesting. I was married and to a woman, which seemed to negate any suggestion I'd end up in a compromising position with anyone on the show. I tried my best but I'm not sure my flirting with Darcey was entirely convincing. I'm also fairly dull. I don't drink a lot, I'd written a book that revealed all of my possible skeletons and I like model trains. Not exactly tabloid fodder. I enjoyed playing with the fact that I was uninteresting and started to play a game to see if I could predict the press stories. For example, on the *Strictly* tour the newspapers were insanely interested in the romance between my fellow contestant Gemma Atkinson and dancer Gorka Marquez. Gemma posted a photo on Instagram of herself giving him a peck on the cheek and the next day the papers were full of headlines about this kiss. Backstage the next night as we were waiting to go on, I suggested to Gemma that we recreate the scene but with me kissing Gorka, and she would stand in the back of shot, looking horrified. It was clearly a joke, and everyone was in on it. I posted it on social media and said to Gemma that I was certain there would be headlines about it the next day. And boy were there. Magazines and tabloids led with the story 'Gemma fumes as Gorka caught kissing mystery woman'. That's what I was – despite being in the tour myself I still wasn't relevant to them. I knew I'd be the mystery brunette one day.

My favourite story that was published was one about myself and Sandi Toksvig. Sandi has been an incredible mentor to me, and a good friend. We don't see each other very often because we're very busy and we live at opposite ends of the country, but I have so much love for her. I learned so much from her sitting at her side on *The News Quiz* and have joined her many times on *QI* as she kicks the ass out of what is a complicated show. She is very fond of me (I don't want to say she loves me as I've never actually gone down on one knee and asked her to marry me) and I think she's brilliant. Anyway, I was informed by a friend one day that an Internet gossip site was running a story that Sandi and I hated each other so much that one of us had got an injunction out on the other. It didn't specify which one of us had decided to take legal action, but it was clearly suggesting that the animosity between us was quite extreme. What was curious was that I was due to appear on *QI* the next week and if she'd taken out an injunction to prevent me from being near her I certainly hadn't been informed of it. Sandi heard about it as well and called me. We decided that the best thing to do was nothing as the story was such utter nonsense, but I still marvel at the fact that it was published. And wonder about the identity of the person who told or sold the story. It was so untrue it was laughable. Is it such an extraordinary thing for two successful women to be friends and support each other? No, but it's probably quite a dull story.

If that kind of thing can be published about me because it's a good, albeit untrue, bit of gossip, why should I believe anything *I* read? But the thing is that people like reading these stories: people buy the newspapers that print them and click on the links to the articles. The negativity that seeps from the Internet creeps to other areas of life. I can now say, admittedly without authority, that the papers will print lies, which turn into tweets, which lead to blogs, which become truths. Unless I'm preparing for a topical comedy show I don't read newspapers anymore. I don't click on headlines. I'm much happier than I've ever been. Apart from that time Sandi Toksvig found me in her bed. That was fun.

It's not just the media who are complicit in increasing negativity. The past couple of years seem to have merged when it comes to the progression of our so-called decision-makers. I returned to *The News Quiz* after almost a year's absence and the email the producer sent to me detailing the stories of the week was almost identical to the one I'd received a year earlier, dominated by Trump and Brexit with peripheral articles on Corbyn and Boris Johnson hanging underneath like perpetual icicles. The repetition wasn't the fault of the producer; far from it – topical programmes reflect the news cycle and that's what people are writing about. But the difficulty of rehashing these stories again and again is that progress is never made, the same conflicts arise and negativity is poured forth.

It's like we're on a treadmill of despair punctuated only by small-scale happiness. The only things we seem to agree on are insignificant and odd. The Natural Environment Research Council ran a poll to name a new ship and the public agreed that the best thing to call it would be *Boaty*

McBoatface. Everyone liked that. But can we sustain our general level of happiness waiting for the next competition to occur? I was unexpectedly cheered, mind you, during a period of recent bad weather to find that gritters have names and you can track them online. Tracking vehicles with names like *Sir Andy Flurry* and *Gritty Gritty Bang Bang* made an otherwise depressing day go much more quickly. I, like many others, feel powerless to change what's happening, and even grassroots political movements struggle at times to make a wholesale impact on those in power.

I try not to make knee-jerk statements regarding those who govern us or who put themselves forward to stand for election. I think it takes a great deal of guts to step forward into the world of politics, far more guts than I possess. People like Jess Phillips and Mhairi Black have spoken openly about the abuse that they see on a daily basis, and they are far braver than I am about stating opinions and opening themselves up to vicious criticism. I believe in democracy, that we have the capacity to vote out those who don't do the job that we want them to do, but at the same time the inequality in the electoral system can lead many to believe that they aren't fully represented by those in power. It's why, in recent times, it appears that even the most unlikely of people can become more powerful than we could ever imagine.

It may be an unpopular statement, but I can completely understand why someone like Donald Trump was elected president. He tapped into that very feeling in America, amongst some, that they weren't listened to, that an elite group of people made decisions and didn't care what happened to the little people. They wanted change and Trump offered that. I'd also like to make it clear at this point that President Trump's politics are about as far removed from mine as it's possible to be, but that doesn't mean I can't see why people voted for him. Inflammatory politics is nothing new and President Trump is exceptionally good at doing what he does. Saying things, whether he means them or not, and then tweeting on to the next topic until he lands on something that works for him. The fact that a man who is as elite as they come, who lied during his campaign, who has been accused of racism and sexual assault and openly mocked people with disabilities, could be elected president of the United States is the best example of the fact that the world has become a place of concern.

Politics is important because it's the root of so much of what happens in society. From the legislation that governs what we can do, to the social and economic policy that sets the agenda for our welfare system, to the taxation that funds public services. And not only that but our politicians are, for me, the outward-facing ambassadors for constituencies and country. The Prime Minister and the cabinet are meant to represent us, and what they do and how they behave is important. There's a remarkable double standard in expecting the electorate to behave in a particular way towards our elected members, when watching Prime Minister's Questions can be less edifying than watching a brawl in a chip shop on a Friday night.

I've thought long and hard about whether or not there's

one identifiable time in our history where things started to go wrong. If I could find one event or person and shout, '*J'accuse!*' at the top of my voice. There are a number of suspects. I think it's tough in Britain to ignore the Thatcher years, but maybe that's because it's the period when I was growing up. Certainly, there was the widening of the gap between rich and poor, the miners' strike, Clause 28, the poll tax, the Falklands War, 3 million un-employed . . . My generation would probably point to that time as the moment we lost our way a bit. But people I've spoken to who are slightly older than I am would suggest that it was the 60s; that free love and hippies and a relaxation of the moral code was the start of the tail-spin. The same argument could be made about the 50s, with Teddy boys and rock and roll, and a younger group might say the Blair years seemed as destructive to them as the 80s did to me.

I don't think there's one obvious moment that we can identify where we stopped being kind and joyous. I think there has always been injustice and cruelty in our lives; it just seems more obvious now than ever. Twenty-four-hour news reporting and online media means that coverage of current affairs is blanket and quite addictive. Back in the day, if you didn't read something in the newspaper in the morning or hear about it on the *Nine O'Clock News*, it didn't happen. Often people would go to bed at night entirely happy not knowing exactly what was happening all over the world at any time. I remember the night that Diana died. I was in a club in Glasgow and someone said that she'd been injured. No one had a phone, or access to a television, so we found an old battery-operated radio that was at the back of a cupboard. We stood around the bar listening to updates because it was the only way to find out what had happened.

Not anymore. Now we can, at the touch of a button, find out all the misery of the world, on a loop, again and again. Donald Trump mocking a disabled reporter during the election campaign. Harvey Weinstein's decades of abuse finally revealed by women willing to stand up to the establishment. The exposure of the lack of equal pay in institutions like the BBC and the corresponding sneering by some men when they learned they were being paid far more than their female counterparts. Racism, sexism, misogyny, homophobia have always been a part of our lives and our history but right now they feel raw and closer to the surface than ever.

Those in power seem to be hell-bent on goading each other and us. #NotAllWorldLeaders obviously, but I have spent a great deal of the past couple of years open-mouthed in astonishment when those elected (and unelected in some cases) snipe at each other with less class than two drunks at a bus stop. When the level of political discourse is set by personal attacks and sound-bite aggression it filters through to all of us. Imagine a teacher sitting down with a modern studies class to show them how democracy works and making them watch an average PMQ. Kids being taught at school not to shout out, not to disrespect others and elected members of Parliament are doing just that. Donald Trump and Kim Jong-un sending missives, often through social media, about nuclear weapons. Goading, bullying, sneering soundbites about things that are desperately important.

So we're surrounded by negativity in the media, with politicians openly goading each other, but those insults on the television rather prove my point. It's cool to be kind because now more than ever, being kind is less popular than being negative. Niche and minority activities are always more edgy than those enjoyed by the majority. Soon, all over the country, kids will stand on street corners with spare 'bags for life', helping people with their shopping and complimenting strangers on their choice of jacket. Kindness speakeasies will spring up, secret underground establishments where everyone is nice.

That's why I'm happy now because I know that I'm finally living my dream of being Molly Ringwald. Maybe you are too? Did you hold the door open for someone today? Did you compliment someone on their hat? Did you help a stranger who was carrying a heavy bag of shopping? If you did then well done. You're the cool kid now. We all are.

CHAPTER 17
TRAVELS WITH MY PLANT: CONTINUED

CAMBRIDGE! It has a university! And it was really lovely.

Sarah Wragg @DrWagg
When my colleague spontaneously bought me a bag of crisps because she knew it would cheer me up. Cheese and onion kindness!

Perfect. Keep a list of things that your friends and colleagues like and buy them those things sometimes. My wife loves a jar of mixed pickles. I buy her one occasionally and she sits on the sofa working her way through them. It's disgusting to watch but she loves it. Sometimes love means letting your partner be disgusting without commenting on it. I always comment on the pickles but I totally try not to.

mizanthrope @lydmizz
I worked @Calais camps. Dozens of msgs of love from children&families to migrants. Usually hidden in pockets of donated clothes.

As I said before, I gave the audience no guidance as to what I meant by an act of kindness. Hence why I've had tweets about crisps and hedgehogs and also stories like this. And all the tales of kindness are valid and lovely. This tweet made me well up though. Members of the public who had donated clothes to those who had nothing is kind enough, but to take the time to send a message of hope was extra special. It probably took less than a minute to scribble something and stick it in a pocket. But the impact may be unimaginable. Beautiful.

Victoria Jane Jones @VicJFenDrayton
Always tell people if they have a label sticking out or something stuck in their teeth, I'd want to know!

This is something we can all do. For goodness' sake, tell them!

Hannah Wilde @justwde
Drunk, missed train, went to buy new ticket woman had special stamp for drunks & validated our expired ticket for next train.

Kindness is sometimes anticipating problems. Well done to whatever train company knew that this was going to happen.

Manchester

Manchester is brilliant. On my first tour I had to cut out a lot of my show because people were laughing so much

I didn't have time to say everything. That's a pretty perfect crowd.

Emma Hawley @MsMeachley
My wife has a baked beans phobia so on the rare occasions I eat them I hide in the kitchen and wash up the second I've finished.

This is considerate kindness, something that is often overlooked. I hate Westerns with a passion, and so my wife will always watch these kinds of films when I'm out. Truth be told, I don't know why I hate Westerns so much. I think it's because they remind me of never-ending Sundays in wintertime when we only had three channels to watch and avoiding a boring John Wayne film was rather difficult. Such consideration is even more valuable when a genuine phobia is involved. My wife hates heights so either we don't go places that are high or I'll ignore her. Not in a bad way – I don't mean I pretend that she isn't there. I mean I don't make her feel bad about her reactions. We went to Barcelona and she insisted that we go to the top of the Casa Batlló to see the view. It was quite early in our relationship and I think she was being brave to try to impress me. It was only when we got to the top that she went a bit funny and sat down. She shuffled round the roof in a seated position and I carried on chatting to her as if nothing was happening. Because making a big deal of it would have made her feel worse. Considerate kindness is wonderful.

Susan Calman

Alice Grey @AlGreeeer
Recently on the train my pasta pesto exploded & in my grease covered frustration, a man simply handed me his napkin & nodded.

I hesitate to talk in stereotypes about this being a very British way to react but it is. Someone's lunch explodes and a stranger steps in to help with just a nod. No conversation needed, no laughter, just an acknowledgement that it could happen to any of us.

Leeds

Leeds is a great place to gig. Although I did have a disappointing cab ride last time I was there. Not knowing the geography and not having had time to check Google Maps, I got in a taxi at the station and asked the driver to take me to my hotel. He drove off and spent a good five minutes wending his way through various one-way systems. He stopped outside a hotel and to my horror I looked across the road and saw the train station. It was directly opposite. He could have told me. He didn't. Bad taxi driver. Or a good one, depending on your view. Perhaps taking advantage of ignorant Scottish comedians is something to be proud of.

Benedict Docherty @docherty5
We rescued a wee black and white cat and have named her Alba – don't tell the landlord . . .

232

You can tell me about all of your secret cats. Please do.
I love the romance.

ktlee @orangespangles
I saved a drowning spider today #actsofkindness

Always save the spiders. Unless it's a giant man-eating
spider and it's attacking you. If that's the case then try and
get away politely. Perhaps try and reason with it. If that
doesn't work then you can use some slight force, yes. But
if it's just a normal household spider then leave it. Or move
it to a comfortable place of safety. My cats like to eat spiders
so I'm often taking them away from the little furry assassins'
reach. I like to think they high eight me afterwards.

Anna Nixon @uniajan
I told my dad how sad I was that I haven't seen many
lambs yet. He then bought me a cuddly toy lamb. I'm
31 yrs old & love it!

Never too old for a gift like that. May I just say to your
dad that I haven't seen any speedboats this year yet?

Liz Hills @LizJHills
would like 2 thank Adam the farmer in Cracoe who
offered 2 look after my friend's bike when he crashed &
was taken 2 hospital.

Thank you, Adam. You did a marvellous thing. If I had
any merchandise I'd send it to you. I have considered a

gift range but I'm not sure how much people would like it. Here are the options:

1. One of those pens that when you turn it upside down something happens. In the old days it used to be ladies whose clothes would come off. I'm thinking of doing one where I'm wearing a duffle coat and when you turn it over the coat comes off and I'm wearing a polo neck. Sexy, right?

2. A range of mugs that only activate when they have a hot drink poured into them. I gave my wife one of these once for her birthday. I didn't tell her I'd taken a picture of me looking awful and she got a fright when she made a cup of tea.

3. Community Action Barbie T-shirts. Although Barbie is a trademark so I'd have to change it. Maybe Community Action Calman. No one would have the guts to sue me!

4. Tea towels with my face on them.

5. Bath towels with my face on them.

6. Keyrings with my face on them, and my nose would light up so they also make a handy torch.

I'll put the links on my website as soon as we get the distribution deals signed.

yoginileeds @yoginileeds
The kindness of hospital staff when my mum died.

I continue to be overwhelmed by the kindness shown
by staff who see us in our darkest hours. Thank you to
each and every one of you.

beccyship @beccyship
Someone stopped me on the street to tell me I had a
train antimacassar stuck to my bum, I was 10mins walk
from station.

I particularly like this tweet because it made me look
up what an antimacassar was. I get great joy from learning
new things.

CHAPTER 18
WE NEED TO TALK ABOUT KEVIN

THE DAY I FELL IN LOVE WITH A MAN

FROM my early teens onwards I've always been in love. Usually with someone I'd never get (unrequited love is my speciality) but always with a woman. Not just sexy love either; I love my friends in a beautiful platonic fashion, but again I don't think I've ever had a really close man friend in my life. It's why, when I met a certain Mr Kevin Clifton, I was expecting to like him, probably admire him, but I didn't expect to fall in love with him. But I did. And I fell hard. I've spent a great deal of time wondering why this happened, why this man made me feel something that no one else ever had. Why was Kevin from Grimsby the man of my dreams? The answer is simple. It's because I'm a human being. And human beings are brilliantly strange, complex and defiant in their unpredictability. Even knowing that at our core we are all terribly strange I was puzzled as to the effect that Kevin had on me, and have spent hours wondering as to the combination of circumstances that might have brought us together. These were not wasted hours, they were times where I felt like one of the great psychiatrists, Freud or Jung or Lucy from the comic *Peanuts*.

Generally I really like people. Not all people of course; there are some terrible human beings on this planet and I've met some of them. But most people are brilliant. Some people are magnificent because they don't even know how wonderful they are. They have no realisation that their very presence on this planet makes it better. And I don't mean the lauded scientists, or the famous musicians. I mean everyday people who go about their business the same as they always have.

I've been fortunate in my life to meet some of the best human beings possible. People who have changed my life for the better. Sometimes these interactions have occurred completely at random. Like the woman who held my hand on a plane because I was frightened. Or the man I met at a party when I was at university who introduced me to the music of Johnny Cash. I'm probably over-analytical about the human condition and can spend hours or even days wondering about what makes us tick. What makes us different and, more importantly, what we have in common. I find other people utterly fascinating, and I'm not ashamed to say that I find joy in almost everyone I meet. Even if I dislike a person I can sit and watch them and wonder that a bundle of connective tissue and organic matter can make me feel the way that I do. I also spend far longer than is necessary thinking about my role and how I interact with people. I'm never wholly satisfied with just knowing someone likes me, I want to know why.

Unless you make a really big effort it's pretty impossible

to live life in isolation. You could buy a cabin in the woods and live a self-sufficient life making clothes from bark, but to my mind that wouldn't be a lot of fun. We need each other for so many reasons and connecting with our fellow humans is crucial. Kindness and joy come from all of us, from the marvellous, magnificent beings that we are. I'm quite lucky because my job as a comedian means that I can't really avoid people, and I wouldn't want to. I have the perfect excuse to meet people, to study them and to learn from them. We are all so very strange and beautiful that I never fail to be amazed by the thoughts and feelings that come out of our brains. From an early age I've marvelled at what makes us who we are, at the strange quirks of humanity on display.

The first time I really wondered about my fellow (wo)man was when I watched a TV show called *You Bet*, which was shown on ITV in the 1980s and 90s. For my international readers, or for young people who may not have experienced the television gold that was *You Bet*, let me try to explain. The basic premise of the show was simple: someone would come on and bet that they could do something. But it was never something dull like 'I bet I can do ten push-ups in thirty seconds'. It was always something magical like 'I can guess the make of a 1900s lawnmower from the sound of the wheels turning', then they'd be blindfolded while someone slowly pushed ten lawnmowers an inch. I find that beautiful. That in a world full of possible interests one person has spent hours listening to a piece of garden equipment.

We human beings, instead of being the source of misery,

can in fact be the source of joy. I've spent far longer than is perhaps necessary wondering about the human condition, considering the process of evolution and thinking about just what it is that makes us human. What makes me who I am, and different from you? Science undoubtedly plays a role, and I know that my genetic make-up plays a huge part in who I am and how I feel about myself. But surely some of what makes us who we are, and what makes us love another human being, can't be scientifically categorised. Sometimes it's just magic.

When I first started on *Strictly Come Dancing* we were taken to some studios in London to film our introductory pieces to camera – the little insert bits, which would help explain who we were to the viewing audience. We were all asked who we would want to dance with and who we would rather not. The only reason I had for not wanting to dance with someone was to do with height: I was pretty sure that dancing with a man two feet taller than me might affect my frame, and my frame was wonky enough to begin with. But when they asked who I did want to dance with, I had only one answer:

Kevin Clifton.

As a long-term *Strictly* superfan, I knew he was the man of my dreams. In a completely non-sexual way, of course. I didn't fancy him, but I did fancy his talent. Let me try to explain that somewhat contradictory notion. I don't want to sleep with men due to the fact I am super-gay and find the idea of hanky-panky with them all wrong. But I do fancy talented men. My mind wants to sleep with them. I know this sounds like a plot from *Black*

Mirror but bear with me. I had watched Kevin dance with his previous partners on the show and I knew he was the man for me. It was like dance Tinder. He seemed patient and kind and he always made his dance partners be the best that they could be. I can honestly say I have never wanted anyone more than I wanted Kevin. Oh, and my wife knows this and is fine about it. We are very modern.

So when they asked me who I wanted, I said him. And I mentioned that I had a picture of Kevin on my fridge. Which I did. And no, I'm not odd, it's a perfectly natural thing to kiss a picture of a stranger in the morning before making coffee. The show obviously loved the idea that I was so besotted with one of the dancers and played with us a bit. Would I get him? Wouldn't I get him? I'm often asked whether or not we knew who our dance partners would be before the show and I certainly didn't. The tears of joy I shed when I found out he was to be my dance boyfriend were absolutely real. I had him! I had Kevin Clifton! He was mine! All mine!

Naturally, all of my 'love' for him was based on entirely superficial knowledge. I'd barely met him, never mind got to know him. And there I was, declaring my love to the nation without a thought for the consequences. I was struck by a terrifying notion: what if he was a complete arsehole? It's happened before. I've really liked someone I've seen on the television and then I've met them, and they are a terrible human being. What would I do if the only man I've ever loved was like that? After the insane rush of the launch we were left, awkwardly saying hello to each other like our mums and dads had made us go to the school dance together. I was paralysed with fear. Kevin of course was more experienced than I was in such circumstances. He'd had a number of previous celebrity partners, although I told him I didn't want to hear about them. Well, you don't want to know about other women, do you? You want to be the special one.

We started dancing. First week was a Viennese waltz to 'Mad About the Boy', which was funny because I was. Looking back, I feel sorry for the poor man. Putting the whole thing into perspective for you, Kevin was up against it.

1. I had never danced before – well, apart from the usual traditional steps we're all forced to learn. At a Scottish school most children learn the noble art of country dancing, generally taught in a lesson called Social Dancing. Social dancing. Perhaps the biggest contradiction I've ever encountered. A smelly gym hall containing a group of prepubescent teens powered only by their overactive hormones, having to touch one another to the sound of accordions. I think it does something to you when your first encounter of what could be considered a sexual nature takes place while a middle-aged woman with a whistle round her neck shouts instructions at you. We learned the classics – the Gay Gordons, Strip the Willow and the Slosh. Sadly, as I got older, I developed a hatred of ceilidhs, much to the disappointment of my English friends, who seemed to think I'd launch into an eightsome reel in my lunch hour at work. The fact is that Scottish country dancing is a more dangerous hobby than juggling chainsaws while being chased by a bear. Done well, a ceilidh is a gentle and dignified event. Badly executed, it becomes, in essence, a woman-throwing competition set to music. But that was the sum total of my dance training. And I wasn't very good at any of it.

2. I hadn't worn a dress or heels since I was seventeen and from what I knew of *Strictly* both of those things were going to feature rather more. Leaving aside the dress horror, my fear of the footwear had a lot less to do with what I would look like and far more to do with whether I would actually be able to walk in them. And even if I managed to get from A to B without falling over, I had to dance in them, which, even with my limited knowledge, I knew would involve some fast footwork and a lot of pain. There's some argument about the origin of this particular quote regarding the Hollywood superstars Fred Astaire and Ginger Rogers, but whoever said it nailed it.

'Sure, he was great, but don't forget that Ginger Rogers did everything he did . . . backwards and in high heels.'

Kevin had never worked with a woman before who had steadfastly refused anything other than brogues or trainers for almost thirty years. Which made everything far more difficult and far slower than it should perhaps have been. And my feet – oh, the pain! The excruciating agony of spending eight hours a day in those tiny stupid shoes made me admire women who do so by choice even more.

3. I hadn't been that close to a man in a very long time. If ever. The first thing I realised, very quickly, about dancing is that you get really, really physically close to someone. Now, while I'm better than I used to be about hugs and stuff, I'm still not the most overly tactile of humans. That doesn't work with dancing. Quite literally one of the first things I had to do was shove my leg in between Kevin's. And it got worse. I had to lean in. Really lean in in the hip region. We had to be connected at all times. Some of you will be reading this and screaming, 'Shut up, Susan, I dream of being slammed against Kevin Clifton for hours every day.' And I know, I had as well. I suppose I just didn't think we would be that close.

4. I got annoyed every time I couldn't do something, and that happened a lot. I would despair of my own inability to move my legs in the right way. It's simple: right, left, back, forward. Yet my tiny legs refused to do what my brain was telling them to. I wanted to be so good, I wanted to prove everyone who thought I would fail wrong; sadly, no one had told my body what the plan was. The first two weeks were, in many ways, disastrous. I wasn't elegant. I wasn't ladylike. I was enthusiastic, but I wasn't what you would call 'good'. I don't take criticism well at the best of times (it's one of my least attractive qualities) and this was, at its heart, a dancing competition. I was going to get criticised by a lot of people. This was going to be tough for both of us.

According to the bookies, Kevin and I were odds-on to go first in the competition and I could see why. As I've said above, I couldn't dance or even walk like a lady and I was probably one of the least well-known names on the show – why would anyone in their right minds pick up the phone to vote for me?

I was torn. This was the show that I'd always wanted to do, but now I was doing it I was terrified. The main source of my fear was simple. I didn't want to embarrass myself. I didn't want to be that person who everyone laughed at. I didn't want to tell Kevin about my fears; I was pretty sure that he wouldn't understand – how could someone so completely talented get why I was a bubbling mess every morning before we trained?

But something very curious happens when you dance with someone for such an intense period. It's like you skip the first two years of a relationship and suddenly land, like an old married couple. One day, in the middle of the second week of training, I started crying and told Kevin everything. And he told me everything. And that was it. It was like I'd known him my entire life and the man I knew was incredible.

He would teach me about the people he admired in dance, showing me videos of Cyd Charisse and Fred Astaire. I taught him about feminism. I think some would say I got the better deal. He thoughtfully choreographed to my strengths, he didn't mind me taking centre stage, he pushed me forward, he built up my self-confidence, he made me laugh more than anyone else ever has.

We went through a great deal together. We occasionally

fought, we definitely cried but he was always there. Every Saturday night before the live show started we would stand on the stairs going up to the studio. Just before Tess and Claudia started the show he would turn to me and say:

'You're awesome, partner. Remember there's nothing you can do that will disappoint me.'

My wife is expected to support me. My friends and family too. But this was someone I hadn't known before, who I'd got to know in the space of a couple of weeks, who was telling me I was amazing. Just before the first show, when I was at my most nervous he said it. It was one of the most shocking and emotional moments I can remember in my life. The man from the television was as nice as he seemed and he was telling me I was great. This grumpy, stooped, sarcastic lesbian thought she was in the middle of a fairytale.

I have no problem in saying that I love Kevin Clifton. My wife has no problem with that either. She has spent years supporting me and trying to build up my confidence but there was only so much she could do because I was afraid to try anything new. Only when I was forced out of my comfort zone did I have to confront my demons.

If I hadn't met Kevin I wouldn't be the person I am now. If I had hidden myself away I wouldn't have had the amazing experiences that I did. That interaction with one amazing man changed my life. On paper we had little in common in terms of our background, but there was a connection. His kindness towards me gave me the greatest joy I've ever experienced. When it comes down to it, being with someone else – whether in a marriage or a weird platonic relationship between a lesbian and a man from Grimsby – is magnificent.

We can study humanity from a scientific viewpoint all we want, but people are the key. Us. The world is full of sparkling gorgeous jewels that we haven't discovered yet. What made that man make such a difference to my life? What was it in him that changed me? I could spend another few months ruminating and considering and investigating. Or I could just accept it and enjoy it.

If I hadn't done something that had frightened me I wouldn't have met him. If I hadn't opened up to him we wouldn't have the relationship we have. We keep in touch, messaging each other about this and that. In week two of *Strictly* I promised I'd get a tattoo that said 'I love Grimsby' on my foot if we got to Blackpool, mainly because I didn't think we'd ever get to Blackpool. But we did, and I got the tattoo. It's on my right foot, which is my best foot, because he taught me to dance and to quite literally put my best foot forward. When I said I'd done it some people on social media suggested I was silly and I could just have let it pass without actually going through with it. But I was always going to get it done. Firstly because I always keep my promises but more importantly because it's a lasting reminder of my time with the boy from Grimsby. Imagine that: getting a tattoo for a man. If there's one example of how a show like *Strictly* can change a girl it's inked permanently on my foot. I love it. Every morning I look at it and it brings me utter joy.

The world is full of Kevin Cliftons; maybe you'll meet

yours. I hope you do, because every night when I went out to dance I knew that there might be 11 million people watching but that one man had my back. My Kevin. The best man a lesbian could fall in love with.

CHAPTER 19
TRAVELS WITH MY PLANT: CONTINUED

TUNBRIDGE WELLS

Lovely place, Tunbridge Wells – or TW as I call it. Actually, I don't call it that. I'm saying that because I forgot to write down notes on the place. Sorry TW. I'll come back soon and pay more attention.

> Sarah Marchant @sarahdoow
> A guy parted a foyer crowd like the Red Sea & led me to the exit as I'm too short to see over a crowd (or anything over 3'10").

Any act of kindness towards short people is always appreciated. For example, if you're a really tall person and you're at the cinema with an average-sized friend, just glance behind you. If the person in the seat behind you appears to be shorter than the average bear, maybe consider swapping seats? Then they won't need to perch on top of the upturned seat like a ten-year-old child.

Edward Pickles @SyringeMonkey
My daughter vomited in the middle of a London theatre.
The souvenir shop gave her a T-shirt. An actress gave
her her trousers!

I love the idea that everyone gave this gentleman's child
an item of clothing so she felt better about herself. Well
done to that actress for donating her trousers. I would do
the same of course. As long as I didn't have to continue
the rest of the show in just my pants. That wouldn't be
positive for anyone.

Stirling

Stirling is always lovely. And as it's only thirty minutes
from my house it was one of the only gigs on my tour
where I could go home after the show. I love you Stirling.

jenni @AitkenJenni
Acts of kindnesss . . . My two year old child stopped
and asked everyone in the park . . . 'hello, how are
you?' . . . only 49 times too many!

This made me smile so much. Being confronted by an
overly friendly child in a park may also be the plot of a
horror movie but I think it would be marvellous.

Jenny Wartnaby @armsofrain
Sweetest old guy gave me 30p to go to the toilet at
Waverley station cos I had no change – 'if you need to
go, you need to go'.

The fact that it costs money to go to the toilet is the source of a lot of my anger in life. I always put in an extra ten pence at such facilities so the person after me only has to pay twenty pence. So make sure you look when you go in. I might have been in before you.

Sheffield

As a lifelong snooker fan, I always love playing Sheffield because the shows take place at the Crucible Theatre. I like to think that one day I'll be back to take on the world's best at potting. I know I won't. You have to keep one leg on the floor at all times in snooker. I don't think you're allowed an Ikea step to help you reach the balls.

> Caitríona Ní Mhurchú @catherine5714
> My doctor kindly rounded my height up to 5'1" on my medical records instead of 5'¼" when I asked her to.

That is definitely kind. Similarly, when I was measured for a medical last year I asked the doctor not to tell me my height. I have said for years that I'm 4'11" but I have a horrible feeling that I might not even be that. She nodded and said, 'Of course I won't tell you. But I wouldn't be upset at being 5'10".' I was most definitely delighted.

> Annette Parker @bogtrottingdog
> I dressed as a squirrel yesterday. Gave an upset small boy a sticker for being a good nut, as I helped him blow up his peach.

stopgo

No idea what the background to this is and quite frankly I don't care. I like to think of Annette randomly dressing up as a squirrel just to make the world a better place. And you do, Annette, you most certainly do.

#themindfulhub @themindfulhub
Kindness – my wife packs lunch every day w little love notes. & the woman who broke into my soup tin when the can thingy broke.

Double whammy. Love notes and some Bear Grylls-style tin opening.

James~ @carlyslaejepsen
I'm here with my lesbian friend whose dad bought us tickets as a coming out present #kindness

This one made me really quite emotional. My parents are absolutely grand with who I am but I was as frightened as anyone else is when I was considering coming out. Buying tickets to my show was an exceptional gesture of acceptance. I'm happy to be anyone's coming-out present.

Alice
Coming to terms with my gender identity, have so many supportive friends lending me clothes and being supportive <3

This wasn't the only tweet I received from audience members coming to terms with gender identity and I take it as an act of kindness that they came to see me. It means more than they can possibly know that my show would be considered a safe space for them. And your friends sound amazing.

Oxford

It has a university! I was also beaten in the *Celebrity University Challenge* semi-finals by a team from one of their colleges! I've forgiven you though. Nearly.

Kate Belcher @KateyBelch

As a primary school drama teacher, giving the most unlikely child the main part in the end of year show.

Yes! This is a life-changing act of kindness. That moment when the person you least expect succeeds in an unlikely way. Having that moment of affirmation and public success could be the start of new self-confidence. That's a brilliant teacher.

Nottingham

Busier than I thought it would be and there were a lot of people on stag nights. Amusingly many of them were dressed up like Robin Hood. I'm sure the residents of Nottingham love it.

tilly branson @tillybranson
My elderly neighbour brings my bin in for me every
week. Every time I thank him he says 'it doesn't cost me
a penny' #kindness

My neighbours bring in the bins for me as well. And I
do it for them. It's a small gesture but one that's most
definitely appreciated.

Jules Pickering @pickering_jules
A year ago we were shopping in Lidl and met a
96-year-old guy who started talking about Spanish onions
to us, we're now friends.

This is a similar story to the one that I started the book
with. The act of opening up a conversation with someone
leading to a friendship you weren't looking for. And I love
the fact that it started over Spanish onions.

Newcastle

What can I say? I've had some of the most extraordinary
times in this city. And I was also thrown out of a shop
for having a fake twenty-pound note on me. Swings and
roundabouts as always.

Charlotte Law @SingUpChar
#Kindness 2 young men sharing my taxi & paying the
fare when metro broke down & I was running late for a
train to London 4 work.

Again and again the small things that we do for each other make an impact. Sharing a cab and paying the fare when you were going that way anyway.

Newbury

It was my first time in Newbury and I wasn't sure what to expect. Turns out Newbury is lovely. Apart from where I stayed. Which was above a nightclub. I wasn't feeling 'loco in Acapulco' at four in the morning.

Laura Birtwistle @ljbirtwistle
Act of kindness, unknown lady paid for petrol when I lost my bankcard and couldn't contact my mum. Never let me pay her back.

I must find that woman and tell her that I can't pay my mortgage.

Steve Madden @steve2cvmadden
True kindness, my wife was born in Iran we have suggested she avoids the family wedding in the USA this year.

This tweet made me laugh and then made me really sad. It's one reason why kindness is so important these days. Cheap air travel has made the world smaller, but sometimes it gets a little too small.

Olivia @mama_pilates
A stranger in a cafe said I was doing a great job of
parenting my young sons on a day when I felt like I was
being useless.

What a smashing compliment to pay someone, and look
how it lifted Olivia's spirit. We never know how people
are feeling inside and one word or gesture can change
everything. I always try to compliment people when I see
them. It's the popcorn effect that gives me joy. A simple
'I heard the show you did last week, I thought it was great'
and their chest puffs out and they figuratively jump two
foot in the air. Very few things give me greater joy than
seeing that kind of happiness.

Milton Keynes

I loved Milton Keynes for many reasons but one of them
was the fact I could open the window in my hotel room.
After six months of travelling on trains, and performing
in theatres and staying in hotels with air conditioning,
there's something truly joyous about being able to open
a window and enjoy some fresh air. I didn't want to leave.
Another slogan for the tourist board: 'Milton Keynes! I
didn't want to leave!' That'll be five hundred pounds,
please.

bettyknowsnothing @100707
Norman just bought us all an ice cream! #kindness

I don't know who Norman is but he's a legend. Imagine buying a group of potential strangers at a comedy show some ice creams. Let's all be more Norman!

Margate

I have a deep and heartfelt obsession with seaside towns and even more so with Victorian architecture. Imagine my joy on my first visit to Margate when I performed at their grand theatre. It was a sweltering hot day and I sat on the beach having an ice cream before the show. I liked Margate.

Laura Kelly @l_kelly73
My mum gave a ticket to see Imelda Staunton in west end play to stranger who had never been to the theatre.

This is a really interesting example of kindness. Because it's not giving someone a gift of something that they know they need. It's giving them an experience that they've not had before. Theatre may not be for everyone but everyone should have the chance to experience it. What a lovely thing to give a stranger.

Em @Miss_ELT
applied for a job. Got rejected. Asked why. Hiring manager said 'it's not you, it's me' #bittersweet #kindness

Whether it's true or not this is a rather kind way of softening the blow. Not only does it take the pressure off the applicant but also it's quite a funny way of doing it.

Rita Wilding @rita_wilding
Daughter suffers from anxiety on trains and one driver noticed her hesitating to board and let her sit in the driver's cab!

What a lovely and kind thing to do. It's also a perfect example of genuinely seeing what someone is feeling. The driver was caring enough to try and help her out and it clearly worked. I'm often struck by the kindness of people who work on public transport because it can be a fractious place to make a living. Overcrowding, late trains and buses and cancellations all contribute to very grumpy passengers. I was on tour and needed desperately to get to my next destination. Not being from round the area, I had no idea that there were races going on in a town along the railway line (Hello Cheltenham!) and arrived at the station to find it packed with very drunk racegoers. I started to panic because unless I got on this train I would have real trouble catching the next train to the town I was performing in. The conductor, like the driver who helped Rita's daughter, spotted me and noted that I wasn't a drunk racegoer. For a start I wasn't wearing a fascinator. The carriages were packed to the brim with people pushing and shoving and I stood back from the train. The conductor took my arm and quietly led me down the train to his cabin just at the back of the driver. He lifted my suitcase in, put his finger against his lips making a 'shhh' noise, and let me sit in his little box for the duration of the journey. He read his paper; I watched the world go by. When I reached my destination I nodded a thanks to him, he nodded back and off I went. What a gent.

Exeter

Exeter was a lovely place. In fact, it's where one member of my audience was incredibly kind to me. After shows I like to come out to the bar to chat or sign books and a woman approached me with a small parcel. She knew that I loved *Doctor Who* and had made me the most perfect TARDIS necklace out of silver. Just because. I now wear that necklace whenever I can, and she tweeted me to say she'd seen it on *QI*. A lovely unexpected gesture that has produced reciprocal joy.

Anna Navas @plymfilmguru
I took my 19-year-old cat Tulip to the vet this week and the vet loved her so much he kissed her. And I cried.

Oh, this story. A vet kissing a cat. It's not what I want my doctor to do but I love a vet who loves animals. I imagine it like an old-fashioned movie, a *Gone With the Wind*-style romance, where the vet turns away but is so overcome with love that he rushes back and snogs the face off the cat. A lot of this is very wrong, I know.

Sarah Haddy @haddys
An American couple bought us dinner when on honeymoon nearly 20 years ago if we did the same to someone else.

This is a gorgeous example of the 'paying it forward' philosophy. Do something nice in the hope that the person will do the same for someone else. I may not put such explicit conditions on such an act of kindness but that's possibly my background as a lawyer. I'd hate to tie someone in to a verbal contract that they couldn't honour. And before anyone tweets me, a verbal contract can be legally binding in Scots law. So there.

Colchester

Colchester was a delight. Really smashing audience and hugely welcoming venue. One of those nights where I was glad to be doing my job.

> Jane Dyster @darcydyster
> I recently went to hospital due to an eye condition I was really worried and the nurse taking my details stopped and hugged me.

I received a number of similar tweets about the NHS. Overwhelmingly people talked about how amazing the staff are, how hard they work and how undervalued they are. Most of all people spoke of the compassion shown by those who look after us at our worst times. How much they value the humanity shown. I've said it before and I'll say it again: those who work for our emergency services do jobs that few of us can do. They are often the ones who run towards danger while we run away.

> KP @KatieAPerfect
> My gf stood up to a racist bigot who was abusing a man

working at Halfords. He then in return fixed her windscreen.

The kindness this tweet refers to is, I think, the fixing of the windscreen. And a kind act it certainly is. But the act of standing up for someone else is kindness personified. It's brave as well. How many of us when seeing something like this would do the same? My wife challenged someone she saw putting up far-right posters in the area we used to live. I believe she said, 'We'll have none of that round here, thanks,' then stood and waited until he left. There's nothing quite like the polite stare of an angry woman to make racists afraid.

Cheltenham

I performed in Cheltenham while the races were on. I've never quite understood the concept of going to the races and getting so drunk that you vomit on yourself. For a start it's rather disrespectful to the horses. They should be the focus of your attention, not whether or not you can neck a bottle of Lambrini in the train toilets on the way there. Anyway, my audience was sober and lovely so that was fine.

Elphie @elphiemcdork
I have difficulties walking and on a train from Bristol to Chelt that was packed with racegoers a woman gave up her seat for me.

Now I'm going to sound old-fashioned here. You should give up your seat for people who need it. I can't stand being on public transport when no one does it. 'But I don't want to offend someone by suggesting that they're old or pregnant,' you cry. Well just ask. They can only say no. And while we're at it, let me answer a frequently asked question from men who have taken the #MeToo and #TimesUp movement as some sort of legal threat to them breathing. Yes, you can still hold a door open for me. You can offer to carry a woman's bags. Just because we don't want to be objectified or sexually assaulted doesn't mean that you can't have good manners.

CHAPTER 20

WHERE IS JOY
AND WHERE CAN I CONTACT HER?

TIPS TO FIND YOUR HAPPY PLACE

I hate the word hero but if you want to call me one I can't stop you. Yes I have, on your behalf, tried out a number of experiments to see if I can make joy happen when we want it to, to see if I can move it into my life artificially. Because while joy can happen quite spontaneously, I'm pretty sure that it can also be encouraged into our lives.

I'm not very good at many things (being dignified, being refined, being tall) but one thing I am good at is experimentation (not like that, quiet down at the back). I like to test things out, keep lists and find solutions to problems. If I've discovered anything in the past few years it's that sitting on my sofa and blaming everyone else for how miserable I am is easy, but lazy as hell. I've looked up lists on the Internet, I've asked friends what makes them happy and I've gone for it. I've experimented using me as the test subject. Which probably makes the whole thing null and void and I probably won't win the Nobel prize for science. Which is disappointing.

So, in no particular order, here are the successful and

Susan Calman

unsuccessful joy-bringing things that I did. If you find these things enjoyable I salute you, and if you shudder at my choices, then that's fine. Maybe open your mind though. Calman joy is everyone's joy.

Shopping

'Let's have a whole day shopping!' my friends exclaim, and my heart sinks. Because they don't mean shopping for SOMETHING, they mean just wandering around touching things but coming home empty-handed. I don't understand the concept of shopping without a purpose. In the same way that I don't get why people like frozen yoghurt; it seems pointless to me. Have some yoghurt **or** have an ice cream. Don't try and make yoghurt into ice cream by keeping it really cold. But I tried shopping as an activity because so many people seem to love it and I hated it. It didn't bring me joy. It brought me excessive unhappiness. The shops were hot, nothing fitted me and everything was too expensive. The best part of the day was when I went home. I tend to shop via the Internet to prevent a temper tantrum in the middle of John Lewis. When I find something I like, I buy five of them so I never have to make a decision; I look like a cross between Steve Jobs and the Men in Black. Shopping in general sucks.

Verdict – NO JOY.

Hill walking

The great outdoors! Or as I call it, 'The big cold green space with nowhere to charge my phone and no television.' So many of my friends like clomping up and down hills

in all weathers and they're always offering to take me
along.

Before I jump right in with my evaluation of this
particular excursion, let me explain that I have a number
of what I believe are quite reasonable objections to climbing
up lumps of earth as a way of chilling out.

1. There is no point to it

Going up a mountain won't magically transport me to
another world, will it? Everything that needs to be done
will still be there when I get back down again! All it
does is delay the inevitable. I wish I could go somewhere
and step through a magic door to another place and
leave my worries behind. If I had the choice I would
teleport myself to Cambodia, which has, statistically, the
shortest population on the planet. I would be like a
giant to them.

But let me clarify this particular objection. I've recently
started going to the gym, so I don't have anything against
exercise per se. My objection is to the nature of that
exercise. I enjoy high-intensity sessions, where for half
an hour you train until you feel like vomiting. Bang! And
the fat is gone. Hill walking is not like that.

You go up a mound of dirt, stop for a bit, and you
come back down again. I don't get it. In the same way
as I really don't 'get' running. In my view you should be
running either to or from something, not 'just because'.
If, at the top of the hill, there was a shop that sold Helen
Mirren merchandise or cowboy hats, I might see the
point. (Although I might suggest to the owner of the

shop that they relocate to their local high street. Due to years of neglect and local authority planning decisions, there are numerous empty units which, with a bit of work, could be a rather more fruitful place to ply their trade than the top of a hill.)

I'm not a scientist but I'm pretty sure that there is an equation involving effort and reward, although that may have been something I saw on *CSI New York*, my least favourite of all of the *CSI* franchise. I know that might seem like superfluous information but what if one day someone asks you that question on, say, *Mastermind*. Then you'll know the answer. You're very welcome.

The problem is that I can't see any logical reason to climb a hill. If I want to look at the world from somewhere high up I can simply get a lift to the top of a tall tower block. Or just look at it on Google Earth on my phone.

2. I have bad memories of hill walking

I was born in 1974 and, like many families at that time, holidayed close to home. The term 'staycation' hadn't yet been coined but that's essentially what we did because my dad always said, 'There's nothing you can find abroad that Scotland doesn't have.' It turns out that, as magnificent a country as Scotland is, this was simply a ruse to prevent us from moaning. In my adult life I've discovered many things in other countries that Scotland doesn't have. Temperatures above 20 degrees in August. Artisan clogs. The Leaning Tower of Pisa. I am absolutely sure that's in Italy, not Arbroath.

But every year we would holiday on Arran, a beautiful

island off the coast of Scotland. And every year we would go walking because if you go to the same small island on holiday for years on end you eventually run out of anything more fun to do. And also, because it's apparently good for young legs to be forced to exercise occasionally. We went walking but we went walking the old-fashioned way. When I was a lad there weren't fancy boots and special kit for children, and even if you'd been able to find such things my parents would have been reluctant to provide such frippery for three under-tens. We made do with what we already had in the wardrobe and so some of my earliest memories involve climbing hills kitted out in wellington boots and, for extra safety, school jumpers. If the forecast suggested bad weather, we would be presented with a pacamac for protection. Unfortunately, as I was the youngest child I always received hand-me-downs. By the time I received the thin cagoule my brother and sister had previously worn, I would have been better off covering myself in cling film and goose fat.

We trudged up a hill in blizzards, had a corned beef sandwich at the top and came back down again. When I asked my parents what the point of it was I was told, 'It's good for you,' which is of course the stock answer every mum or dad gives when they can't give a good reason why their child should do something. 'Why do I need to eat peas, Mum?' Because they're good for you. 'Why do I need to go to bed this early, Mum?' Because it's good for you. 'Why do you need a gin and tonic while you're ironing, Mum?' Because it's good for you.

3. Toilets (or lack thereof)

I'm paranoid regarding toilets. Every time I go somewhere new, I'm terrified that either no toilets will be available or that the toilets will be of a poor standard and each have their own particular brand of terror attached to it. When it comes to the outdoors, it's the former issue that concerns me most.

It would seem that the majority of hill walkers object to the construction of lavish lavatories at convenient fifteen-minute intervals and that terrifies me. I drink a lot of water because I'm frightened of not drinking enough water and becoming dehydrated because I once read an article about the dangers of becoming dehydrated. I try to ensure that, at all times, I'm never more than fifteen minutes (which is the maximum time my pelvic floor can hold out) away from facilities.

I have an unhealthy preoccupation with the water closet, which comes from my mother (naturally). She told me when I was younger, 'Always go to a toilet when you see a toilet because you never know when you're going to see another toilet.' Can't walk past one now. Going to the buffet car on a train can be a two-hour trip.

It would not be an exaggeration to say that needing the toilet and there not being one available is probably my greatest fear. Above raisins, flip-flops and finding a spider in a pack of bananas. That last phobia appeared fairly recently after reading too many articles on the Internet. It seems that every week there's another report of a tropical arachnid appearing in an unsuspecting shopper's purchases. I'm prepared for such eventualities.

If I buy a bunch of bananas now the first thing I do is throw them on the floor to stun any potential threat, then open the packet with a pair of tongs in one hand and a newspaper in the other. I will not be a story in *Take a Break* magazine. And no I won't buy them loose, who knows who has touched them.

The only thing you can do if you're in the great outdoors and you need to go is to squat behind a bush or a tree or some other natural barrier. Not only is it undignified but also there are clear health and safety issues. Everyone knows that you mustn't stray too far from the group you're with when on a hike. There are two instances when humans are at their most vulnerable, firstly when asleep and secondly when urinating. I don't want to be attacked by a bear while my trousers are down. And before you say it, I know that supposedly there are no bears indigenous to the United Kingdom. But they haven't been to the right parts of Soho.

I don't care how well you know someone, a toilet door is vital to maintaining a friendship. You shouldn't pee within earshot or within the vision of anyone else. The only time it is acceptable to go to the toilet when someone else can see you is if you are trapped in a lift.

4. Food

Eating is the second most important thing in my life after toilets. Which is nicely cyclical if you think about it. At the start of any day I need to know what I'm eating and when I'm eating it. I plan breakfast, lunch and dinner every day. If I'm going out for dinner I look up the menu of the restaurant and choose what I'm having in advance. I ignore any specials because that's just gambling with enjoyment. The worst possible place on the planet for me is somewhere with no cafes or shops in case I get hungry. I went hill walking with my friend Muriel to see if it would make me happy, and knowing I would be at least three hours away from the nearest Marks & Spencer, I stocked up in advance of the expedition. Sandwiches, crisps, chocolate, drinks. Vol au vents were probably not the most practical snacks to take but there's no need to turn into an animal, is there? My rucksack ended up being larger than me and there was a clear and present danger that if I fell over I would be stuck on my back like a struggling turtle.

The best part of the day was when we went home.

Verdict – LOTS OF JOY IF I'M WITH A FRIEND, NO JOY REGARDING THE WALKING BIT. MAY AS WELL MEET THE FRIEND IN THE PUB.

Holidays

Lots of people say that there's no greater joy in life than getting away from it all on holiday. I fundamentally disagree. Even when summertime arrives, the few weeks when I throw off my winter wardrobe of duffle coat and wool polo neck and throw on my summer wardrobe of linen duffle coat and cotton polo neck, I refuse to acknowledge the possible joy that might occur. I don't like the heat, the excessive exposure of body parts and, most depressingly, the pressure to have fun with friends.

Of course I have friends, and not just ones on Facebook either. Proper friends, some of whom I've met on more than one occasion. But even though I am, and have always been, surrounded by lots of lovely people in my life I've never, ever been on holiday with any of them. You know, on one of those holidays you read about in magazines or see on BBC Three where ten or so mates go abroad and drink lots and get up to high jinks. And I'd never really thought it was unusual until I was swapping holiday stories with a colleague recently. She was utterly horrified that I'd never had that bonding experience of painful sunburn and vomiting into a swimming pool.

If I'm honest the main reason I've never had that brand of fun is, quite simply, that no one's ever invited me. I don't write that to elicit sympathy (although feel free to make soothing noises while you're reading this), it's simply the truth. But why would such a gregarious, funny, charming woman (that's me, by the way) be excluded from this rite of passage experienced by so many? I think there are a number of reasons:

1. In my twenties I was the only lesbian in my group of friends. Thinking back, I wonder if some of my mates thought I'd make them listen to me reading *Oranges Are Not the Only Fruit* out loud round the swimming pool while they were trying to get laid.

2. I organise too much. If you want a relaxed holiday I'm not your woman. I suspect friends got the vibe that if I was to accompany them they would get a laminated itinerary in the post the next morning. Apparently, some people don't want that.

3. I get up every morning at about 6 a.m. It's a curse. I've never been able to sleep in. Apparently, some people don't want that either.

4. I can only spend a maximum of one hour at a time in the sun before I get bored and need attention. Sunbathing is, to me, the most boring of all activities. I need regular outings. Mainly those specified on the laminated itinerary.

5. I'm weird. I need to eat every four hours. I won't drink water out of jugs. I'm frightened of sandwiches if I haven't made them myself. I need to check the health and safety ratings of any accommodation. I can't go to the toilet if there's someone within hearing distance. Flip-flops make me feel sick. And so on, and so on, and so on.

It doesn't matter. I didn't want to go on holiday with other people anyway. I know that makes me sound awful, but I like my friends, you see. I don't want to spend two weeks trapped in an apartment block with people I previously liked, seething with resentment about the fact they didn't change the toilet roll when it ran out. My friends and I are suited to weekends away together, probably in the autumn, definitely in Scotland, where we can watch box sets of *Doctor Who*, drink some pink champagne and then go back to our own homes.

So what if I don't have stories of a fortnight of bonding! I have friends. Some of them have lasted twenty years with me. And that definitely wouldn't have happened if we'd gone away together. So, while I look at photos on Facebook of friends who are having just the best time together in hot tubs and on beaches, I'm sitting in my house alone. That makes me happier than anything.

Verdict – NO JOY. STAY AT HOME INSTEAD.

Extreme sports

Many of my friends like to do dangerous things like bungee jumping or cave diving or eating raw pasta, but I've never been a fan. I don't like the feeling of fear, mainly because it's so, well, frightening. But as part of this experimentation process I tried to separate my rational mind from my fears. Friends tell me that they get joy from such activities because of the immediate surge in adrenaline and endorphins, which tricks their brain into experiencing joy in a surge of fear-filled happiness.

I was intrigued; maybe this was a short cut. Perhaps the way to cheer up the nation was to dangle everyone from a great height for five minutes on a Monday morning whether they liked it or not. I investigated what I could do to get that feeling of being scared stupid. Perhaps skydiving, or driving a racing car; perhaps I could abseil down a tall building.

I decided not to. Partly because the last time I did something on the extreme end of the spectrum it went badly wrong. I agreed to do a zipslide over the River Clyde in Glasgow. The starting point was at the top of something called the Finnieston Crane. It's a giant disused cantilever crane that used to be used to load cargo onto ships and now stands as testament to the city's industrial heritage. I said I would do the slide because it was for charity and I didn't know anything about it. That's what I used to be like when I was younger. Not afraid of anything until I found out differently. What a fool. I was fine about the whole thing; even when I was standing at the bottom of the 53-metre-tall structure I was pretty blasé about it. You just step off and gently slide across the river. How cool would I look? Like James Bond but better.

It was only when I was walking up the many, many steps to take me to the top that I realised just how high up I was going. As the ground disappeared I started to sweat a little. The higher we went the more my stomach started to cramp. I didn't want to do it. But I was one of a number of people walking up the stairs and everyone else seemed absolutely fine about it all. I reached the top and rather than say, 'Please can I go home now?' I allowed myself to be strapped into the harness. As I stood at the top of the crane and looked down, all I wanted to do was scream. And not in a joyous, fun-loving way – in a way that made it very clear that I believed I would die. I stepped off the crane and slid to the other side in complete silence. I unbuckled the harness and walked over the bridge to the bottom of the crane where I had started. It was at that point that I violently vomited without a break for about five minutes. I was crying at the same time, which made breathing difficult, and I started to choke, so the organisers of the charity event moved me out of the way as I was putting off others who had signed up to help. It was at this point that I realised I wasn't cut out for extreme activities. The most extreme behaviour I'll ever exhibit is cutting it a bit fine for a dinner reservation, or not packing a spare pair of trousers when it might rain or wearing a blue belt with a pair of black trousers.

Verdict – NO JOY. JUST VOMIT.

I wanted to stop these experiments mostly because I was trying to force happiness into my life and that's not true joy. Instead of trying to do what other people insist makes them happy I decided to tell you what makes me happy. You may not understand some of these things because they're very personal. And I've not included many specific joy-providing moments because I can't recreate them. One of my earliest memories of joy was sitting in the family home when I was about ten. It was a warm summer's day, not too hot and not too cold, and I think I'd been out in the garden. I was pleasantly tired, and for dinner we had ordered a curry. I had the loveliest chicken korma (I was too young for very spicy food), which was the most gorgeous thing I'd ever tasted. There was a strange version of Agatha Christie's *And Then There Were None* on TV. I've since tracked it down and watched it again. Made in 1974 and starring, amongst others, Charles Aznavour and Oliver Reed, it's an odd adaptation but at the time, having no comparator, it seemed like the most compelling bit of drama I'd ever seen. I remember that evening as if it was yesterday. Pure happiness and joy. All I did was have dinner and watch TV with my family but something about it all made it special. I have tried to recreate that feeling but it doesn't work. I even tracked down the DVD and ordered a chicken korma. I had a pleasant evening, but it wasn't the same as I remembered – partly because my family wasn't there and mostly because I'm no longer ten. Sometimes the memory of the moment provides more joy than trying to recreate it.

Some things, however, are guaranteed to make me joyful. Try them if you want. But don't blame me if you hate them. You might prefer to zipslide off a crane.

1. Going into a restaurant with a signed celebrity photo in the window, especially if the celebrity is someone like Gary Lineker or an old-time soap star. I know that I will enjoy eating anywhere that thinks this endorsement will entice people in. They deserve my custom. I also find great joy in the way that they display the photographs as if they're the best things in the world. One of my ambitions is to go into a restaurant and have them ask to take a picture of me. Next time I walked past, my photo would be in the window. I'd love that. That would bring me more joy than anything.

2. Animals make me happy. All animals make me happy but you may have picked up that cats, specifically, bring me the most joy and I currently have five of the furry creatures. My little cats Muppet and Oscar, who I've written about before, sadly passed away last year so my wife and I thought 'Let's get some more kittens.' In my view my house isn't a home without lots of felines running about. We always adopt rescue cats and so we phoned the cat protection and said 'can we have some kittens, please?' They said 'yes, we just need to send round the cat social workers.' It was one of those conversations where I worried if my hearing was going, so I said, 'I'm sorry, I may have misheard you, did you say "cat social workers"?' As Jeremy Hardy said to me, how do they train cats to be social workers? They don't have any thumbs, they can't hold a clipboard . . . it doesn't make any sense.

They told me that they would send the cat social workers round the next weekend to check out the house and see if we were appropriate adopters. I was terrified! What if I wasn't approved for more cats? It would be like telling Piers Morgan that he wasn't allowed to be a wanker. The only time I've been more terrified is when I paid £500 – that's right, £500 – to a cat psychiatrist to come to my house because one of my cats looked a bit sad. I'm a fanny. Anyway, I cleaned the flat from top to bottom, put out some Mint Viscounts (posh biscuits reserved for important visitors), told the existing cats what to say to the cat social workers and luckily, we were approved. We now have: Pickle Kylie Joyce Grenfell, Daisy Fay Harper, Olivia Pope, Dr Abigail Bartlet and DCI Jane Tennison.

The names are carefully chosen from a list of strong female role models and I love them. I'm sure others are less keen on our eccentrically named brood, though. One of the best moments of my life was when I registered those cats at our vet's. They had been seen by a medical professional previously but under their birth names. This was the moment where they became ours, and I needed to formally record their new monikers. I walked into the surgery and informed the nurse on the desk that we had adopted some new kittens and that they were the most special little puddings in the world. She opened up the computer and started to type. As expected she asked what the cats were called and so I started to list them. She typed them in, blinking slowly, until I reached the last two cats to be registered. 'Daisy Fay Harper and DCI – that's short for Detective Chief Inspector – Jane Tennison. Tennison with an I not a Y.' The nurse took a deep breath and quietly asked, 'Should I call her DCI Tennison when she comes in for treatment?' I nodded with more vigour than was necessary and said, 'She's worked hard for recognition and she should be addressed by her full rank. Thank you.' She nodded back at me and closed the computer. To be fair to her she managed to wait until I was outside before she started laughing.

The first time I took my furry police inspector to the vet was truly gorgeous. The vet walked out, glanced at her notes and to her credit looked me straight in the eye and shouted, 'DCI Jane Tennison?' I jumped up, cat carrier in hand and exclaimed, 'She's here, it's Saturday, she's out of uniform!'

Those cats bring me so much joy. We always adopt the ones that no one wants. One has anxiety, one has a heart murmur and one can't work out stairs. I call our house The Calman Home for Wayward Girls. And I love them.

Anatole France wrote, 'Until one has loved an animal, a part of one's soul remains unawakened.' And he was right. Animals bring joy to my life every day.

3. I love model trains. To be honest, I love anything miniature. I don't know why. From a very early age I've always been fascinated by things that are tiny. And yes, I know I'm short, very funny, but that's not the reason I like tiny things. It's the detail; it's the fact that someone has taken the time to make something perfect that's a precise scale model of something else. Because there's absolutely no reason to do it. As I've got older I've rediscovered my love of such things and decided I'd like to start collecting small things. I told my wife, who always moans that I'm incredibly difficult to buy presents for, that I'd like to start collecting doll's house furniture. She looked at me with some concern and fumbled around the subject for a while before coming out with the question that clearly concerned her. Did I want a doll's house? I told her categorically that I wasn't a weirdo, I didn't want a doll's house, I just wanted a tiny Chesterfield, or a tiny biscuit tin. Still confused by my perfectly reasonable request, she asked what I'd do with all my miniature furniture. I told her I'd put it in a display cabinet and then occasionally take the pieces out and look at them. She left the room at that point. I'm expecting big things for my birthday this year. Or not so big!

I dream of having a model train. But that dream is about far more than simply building a train track in my attic. The joy I seek has its roots in a childhood memory.

When I was about ten my mum would drive us to school every morning. We used to pass a house that was on the corner of a street with its fence curving round to reveal a circular garden. The front of the house was quite plain as I recall, with a fairly uninteresting strip of earth outside it that followed the curve of the fence. One day we were driving past and I realised that it was far more than that; the strip of earth was a track and on it ran a train. This was a model train, clearly, but it was big enough to sit on. The owner of the house was travelling round in a circle, at eight o'clock in the morning. He looked like the happiest man in the world and, from the moment I saw that man on that train, I've wanted that joy. I know that if I could have a sit-on train in my garden I would find that joy. I want a train that stops at the front gate. I'll collect guests and take them up the driveway. And yes, before you ask, I will have several outfits ranging from dungarees to full dress uniform. I think it will bring me more happiness than anything else in the world. My wife might leave me but that's OK. I'll have my train to sit on.

4. Being in my house is the source of almost all of my joy in life. I love it. I love sitting in my pants watching box sets. It's not the most interesting life but damn it, it's mine. Add to that good food and the occasional glass of beer and I'm set. People who make me laugh are welcome, people who let me cry even more so. Friends and family and cats. It's all I need.

The act of writing about things that make me happy has made me smile. I suppose it's the old-fashioned 'count your blessings' idea, isn't it? If you're feeling the absence of joy in your life maybe try to make a similar list. It really does help in moments where things seem a little grey to think about the good things that I have. A house, my wife, the cats and one day a train I can sit on. You can drive past my house and see me on it. I bet I'll look amazing.

CHAPTER 21
AND IN THE END........

SO, this is it. The end of the book. The conclusion. This is where, according to the traditional structure of a piece of non-fiction, I would tie everything up neatly in a bow, leaving both you and me satisfied at the end of our journey together. It's the reason why I love traditional, middle-of-the-road crime fiction and drama. You never finish an Agatha Christie without knowing whodunnit, do you? There's an implied contract that at the end of a book or television adaptation the killer will be presented to you at the denouement in a satisfying dining-room accusation scene.

And I know how frustrating it is when there isn't a decent conclusion to something. I watched a film with Jake Gyllenhaal recently called *Enemy*. I won't spoil it for you, but I needed to watch a YouTube video and read an article to understand what it was about. And even after that I'm not entirely sure what I watched. I do know that those two hours could have been spent doing something more fun, like giving my bins a good scrub. If you're

intrigued about that film now I've given it such a build-up let me give you one piece of advice. Don't watch it if you're on a date in the early stages of a relationship. My wife and I had an epic argument after we saw it, not just about what the film was about but also the fact that she had made me watch it and I hated her for that.

Anyway, the point is that my conclusion to this book may be disappointing in that I don't have a solution. This is a choose-your-own adventure and it starts now. I believe that we need to be kinder and we definitely need to celebrate joy more. But I can't physically come into your house and make you nicer and happier. I'd love to, like a tiny Scottish happy Santa. But I just don't have the time, and quite frankly it's against the law to break into someone's house, whatever the rationale behind it. So, it's up to you. I'd love this to be a book that spurs people into action, and that you think of me next time you're in a situation where you have to make that split-second decision whether to be kind or not. The next time you feel that surge of joy you remember my face. Actually, now I've written that last sentence it sounds a little bit odd. Think of me if you feel joy, as long as it's not in a sexy, pervy way. That's not what I want my legacy to be.

I want this to be a wonderful world. I want it to continue to be a place where magnificent, odd, eccentric individuals flourish. I need it to be better for those who come after us. I'm going to do my absolute best, even if I fail along the way.

To kick-start my new lease of life I needed a sprinkle of glitter, and the sparkle of sequins. Maybe this book might change your mind, or at the very least help you see joy in new places. If it does then I hope you'll join me in a peaceful revolution to change the world. We meet at 6 p.m. on a Monday in a quiet park. Bring snacks. But nothing with jam in it. I hate jam.

This is a Calman Revolution. Small, but determined.

This was my Calmanifesto.
I hope you enjoyed it.

EPILOGUE

I'M sitting in my study in Glasgow looking out of the window. My house overlooks a park and I spend a great deal of my day just watching people go about their business (not in a creepy way, honest). There is a theory that the act of being watched makes you a better person. For example, if you know that someone can see you, you're less likely to drop litter or commit some other such anti-social act. I think that's why I like watching the people in the park when they don't know I'm there. They behave in keeping with their true nature. I can also watch the seasons change and the world turn slowly. In the summer it's full of sunbathers and children playing. In the snow it's covered in the footprints of children running to sledge down the hills. Even on those dark winter nights it's a pleasure to peer into the gloom. Dog walkers attach different-coloured lights to their pets' collars which, when they run around in the evening, means I'm treated to a private light show that wouldn't look out of place in Las Vegas.

I sit here and think and write, and the park makes me happy. I listen to music when I write and find that blue-grass and country are perfect for their rhythm and tone. I drink a damn fine cup of coffee from a mug that someone lovely gave me, I look at a tiny dachshund chasing a Labrador up a hill in the park and I listen to a song about campfires and lost love. It makes me smile.

Small things. Tiny pockets of joy. Remembering kindness. Being nice. It's simple but glorious to be happy.

Even if the world doesn't change, I'm not going to stop trying.

Because we're worth it.

ACKNOWLEDGEMENTS

THIS book couldn't have happened without the support of many people. In fact, the past year or so would have been a nightmare without them. If you're reading this and think 'What about me, Calman?' I'm sorry if I've not named you. Forgive me.

This book has been a joy to write thanks to a few people. Lisa Highton, my editor, who calms me, supports me and makes me feel like a million dollars. Everyone at Two Roads who had faith in me from my first book. Vivienne Clore, agent to the stars (and me), who continues to kick ass in every way and is the source of great joy in my life. Especially when she sends me emails with the subject 'I'll tell them to piss off shall I?'

Thanks also to Ben Summers for his cute crabs on *Cheer Up Love* and the adorable sunshine in this book. His artwork brings life to the things in my head. And eternal gratitude to Rosie Gailer and Emma Petfield, who help this book reach as many people as possible, while dealing with my fear of publicity. Thank you for your patience.

My girl squad of Muriel Gray, Jo Rowling, Val McDermid, Jenny Colgan and Emma Kennedy who sent messages of support every dancing day to me. They are the ultimate superheroes. Also thanks to all my friends who inspire me – Millican, Ryan, Pascoe, Fostekew, Toksvig, Perkins, Hagen, Christie and more.

My lovely family, who are amazing. They've put up with a lot in the past and they'll put up with a lot more. My cats, who keep me company when I write. I love them almost more than any human in my life.

Kevin, of course, and everyone at *Strictly*, who made my time there a joy.

And finally, my wife, Lee. A supporter like no other who spent every weekend on a train to London to sit and watch me dance. The kindest person I know and the source of all the joy in the world. All of it. It's all from her. I will be your Saturday Susan every night.

ABOUT THE
AUTHOR

Born in Glasgow, Susan Calman escaped corporate law to become a Stand Up Comedian. She's a regular on radio and television shows like *QI* and *The News Quiz* and has presented the shows *The Boss* and *Armchair Detectives* as well as the recnt travel documentary series, *Secret Scotland*. She recently appeared on *Strictly Come Dancing* where she made it all the way to Week Ten. Even more excitingly she won the Glitterball on the *Strictly Live* tour. An advocate for LGBTQ+ and mental health issues, she lives with her wife and cats in Glasgow.

Enjoyed *Sunny Side Up?*

You can read, or listen to, Susan's first book ...

CHEER UP
LOVE

Adventures in depression with the
CRAB of **HATE**

'Susan Calman never fails to make me hoot with laughter'
Sarah Millican

'Heartbreaking and heart-warming . . . Avoiding all the usual "tears of a clown" clichés, she tackles homophobia, self-harm and finding your voice. Unmissable'
Damian Barr, *Metro*

'Deeply personal and painfully honest but funny'
The Times Scotland

'Fantastic, funny, moving . . . A perceptive look at depression – with added laughs'
Viv Groskop

'Calman's account of depression, though deeply honest, is surprisingly hilarious and uplifting'   *The Pool*

'There are so many depressing books about being funny, so it's refreshing to read a funny one about being depressed. I have never laughed quite so heartily at someone else's genuine distress – which I hope is her intention'

Miles Jupp